FACING FORGIVENESS

A well tried remedy for what seems to be ailing society in a big way—forgiveness.

Most Reverend John Favalora
Archbishop of Miami, from the Foreword

A heartrending and inspiring collection of stories drawn from personal experiences, reminding us that "Christian forgiveness is about remembering, not forgetting." *Facing Forgiveness* is an excellent and practical resource for all who struggle to forgive and for those accompanying others on this sometimes painful, but ultimately freeing journey.

Edith Prendergast, R.S.C.
Director of Religious Education, Archdiocese of Los Angeles

In an era when the capacity to forgive seems pushed to its limits, this eloquent book radiates much needed hope. These touching and powerful stories are required reading for the heart. *Facing Forgiveness* is an interactive work of the best practices for a healthy and whole spiritual life.

Br. Joel Giallanza, C.S.C.
Vicar for Religous, Diocese of Austin, Texas, and author of *Source and Summit*

The down-to-earth stories are gems that show the reader what forgiveness means and how to choose it. Filled with practical wisdom, this is an ideal resource for personal spiritual growth and small group reflection.

Sheila Garcia
Secretariat for Family, Laity, Women, and Youth, U.S. Conference of Catholic Bishops

This exceptional book describes how real lives are changed by a person's ability to forgive, the true essence of Christianity. A must-have resource for all pastoral ministers, parish teams, caregivers, and grief groups.

Linda Amadeo, R.N., M.S.
Executive Editor, *Human Development* magazine

Facing Forgiveness is a truly uplifting work that will draw the reader into the beauty and importance of forgiveness. This book should serve as a way for many people to heal from deep injustices against them.

Robert Enright
Professor of Educational Psychology, University of Wisconsin-Madison

FACING FORGIVENESS

A Catholic's Guide
to Letting Go
of Anger and
Welcoming
Reconciliation

Loughlan **Sofield**, S.T.
Carroll **Juliano**, S.H.C.J.
Bishop Gregory M. **Aymond**

ave maria press A m P notre dame, indiana

With love and gratitude to:
Eleanor Doyle and Georgeanna Juliano
Ray and Barbara Sofield
Yvonne and Louis Aymond

Biblical epigraphs at the opening of the chapters are from the *New Revised Standard Version of the Bible*, copyright © 1993 and 1989 by the Division of Christian Education of the National Council of Churches of Christ in the U. S. A. Used by permission. All rights reserved.

Other biblical quotes are from *The New American Bible* copyright © 1991, 1986, and 1970 by the Confraternity of Christian Doctrine, Washington, DC, and are used by permission of the copyright owner. All rights reserved. No part of *The New American Bible* may be reproduced in any form or by any means without permission in writing from the publisher.

Excerpts from the English translation of *Rite of Penance* ©1974, International Committee on English in The Liturgy, Inc. (ICEL). All rights reserved.

Founded in 1865, Ave Maria Press is a ministry of the Indiana Province of Holy Cross.

www.avemariapress.com

ISBN–10 1-59471-122-4   ISBN–13 978-1-59471-122-0

Cover and text design by John Carson

Printed and bound in the United States of America.

CONTENTS

Part III: The Sacrament of Penance and Reconciliation

Appendices

FOREWORD

There seems to be more than enough anger to go around these days. It's as if there's something in the water. Nightly on television we witness the horrible violence that pervades our urban centers, and that has now, sadly, reached our once placid rural areas. It is on the screen, in the music, in our schools, in our homes. A lot of people have a lot of anger.

The sad thing is that most angry people don't know that they are angry, and if they do, they don't know what to do about it. *Facing Forgiveness* is a very helpful examination of conscience with moving personal testimony on behalf of letting go of anger and welcoming the gift of healing through forgiveness. Some people need professional assistance to deal with their anger, but most people don't need to face a psychiatrist, they need to face themselves.

Christians have the ultimate example of forgiveness in Jesus on the cross. This refreshing book is filled with numerous stories illustrating how forgiveness is also happening today all around us. It invites the reader to discover or rediscover what the Church through its sacrament of reconciliation has taught and preached down through the centuries. Every sincere penitent knows the treasure that forgiveness is for the spirit. It is resurrection; it is life.

I salute this talented Brother, Sister, Bishop Team for authoring this book about a wise, down-to-earth, practical, well-tried remedy for what seems to be ailing society in a big way—forgiveness.

Most Reverend John Favalora
Archbishop of Miami

ACKNOWLEDGMENTS

This book is possible because of the generosity of so many people, especially those who over the years shared their profound, sacred stories of forgiveness with us. We will be forever indebted to you. Your stories have been the source of hope to so many. Special appreciation goes to those who allowed us to share their stories of hope: Kathy Anderson, Tom Butler, Stancil Campbell, April Dunham, Loris Nickel Edwards, Bob and Judy Goetz, Diana and Luc Papillon, and Bishop Willie Walsh. This book would not have been possible without the support and contribution from each of you.

We especially wish to express our deep appreciation to those who submitted chapters: Dawne Fleri, Anne Hansen, Christy McMurren, Monsignor Michael Mulvey, and Helen Osman. We are also grateful to the publishers who granted permission for us to use certain stories.

This book would not have been possible without the assistance of Father Gary Banks, S.T., Doctor John Brun, Monsignor Ronny Jenkins, Linda Miller, Matthew Mumaugh, Father Louis Murphy, S.T., and Father Kevin Rai.

Finally, we would like to express our gratitude to the staff of Ave Maria Press, especially Bob Hamma, whose advice, assistance, encouragement, and friendship have given us the support to complete this book.

INTRODUCTION

This book grew out of the experience of conducting workshops on anger and forgiveness, teaching, and serving as pastoral counselors. During these workshops, classes, and sessions, we listened to the pain and joy of people who approached us to talk about pastoral, personal issues. The issue of forgiveness is like a magnet that draws people into its field. It is striking how many people willingly share personal stories of forgiveness and non-forgiveness. Those who shared the stories of forgiveness had experienced, almost to a person, a rebirth, an over-powering sense of new life.

Conversely, those who had made the decision to hold on to their anger and not forgive continued to bear the weight of non-forgiveness. Sadly, some reported their inability to forgive someone who was long dead, never realizing that it was not hurting the offender, but was causing the non-forgiver eternal grief, physical trauma, and at times, clinical depression. In the retelling of these stories of non-forgiveness, ambivalence is evident. These people struggle with the desire to be free of the burden on the one hand, while also desiring to nurse the offenses of the past. They cannot tolerate the personal pain they are experiencing in holding on to the evils of the past, yet for reasons sometimes unclear even to themselves, they cannot bring themselves to forgive.

In the pastoral counseling sessions, we have had the graced opportunity to walk with those on the journey to forgiveness as they arrived at a point where, with God's grace, they chose forgiveness and life. Forgiveness is neither a cognitive nor an emotional response. Forgiveness is an act of the will. It is the choice to let go of the desire to get even with an offending party. During counseling sessions, those who chose forgiveness experienced a profound sense of freedom and would often describe it as if a physical, emotional, and spiritual weight had been lifted from their shoulders.

Forgiveness is a topic that is always relevant. It is particularly relevant today. Our generation seems to value revenge more than mercy. Too often, television shows and movies foster violence, disrespect, revenge, and the devaluing of others. Many talk shows, which may at some level mirror the values of our society, more frequently extol greed, anger, revenge, and personal violence than forgiveness, reconciliation, and compassion.

We have dealt with some of the issues of forgiveness in two previous books, *Design for Wholeness* and *Building Community*. This present book builds on the two previous ones.

Part I invites you to begin the journey of forgiveness by discerning your personal beliefs about and experiences with forgiveness. Our beliefs are included to serve as a catalyst to help you to reflect on and articulate your beliefs about forgiveness. These initial chapters serve as a background to explore the faces of forgiveness presented in Part II.

Part II is the heart of the book. The chapters included in this section attempt to put human faces on a psychological and theological concept. You will read a sampling from the many overwhelming stories of forgiveness that it has been our privilege to hear. You will also hear the sad stories of some who have chosen the course of non-forgiveness. Some of the stories are of almost epic proportions, and some convey their power through their simplicity.

In this section, you will meet such fascinating people as Bishop Willie Walsh of Killaloe, who models Church leadership in the midst of the sexual abuse crisis. The stories of Johanna, Nigel, Christine, and Luc will challenge you to forgive those whom you thought it would be impossible to forgive. Mary will invite you to look into the eyes of your tormentors. April will teach you how to forgive yourself and choose new life. These and the other people you will encounter in this book will provide an opportunity to look in awe into the faces of forgiveness.

The main reason why people choose to retain their anger and not forgive is, as they declare, "I don't know how to forgive." They may not know how to forgive because they lack human models of forgiveness. Hopefully, these stories will provide you with tangible, concrete models of forgiveness.

May this journey of forgiveness that you will experience as you read these stories lead you to pray for the grace to forgive; whether that is forgiveness of self or forgiveness of others; whether it is forgiveness in the present or forgiveness for actions in the past. We believe that God will offer the gift of forgiveness.

Personal reflection questions are included after each vignette to help you to clarify your own beliefs and attitudes about forgiveness. We have included a scripture quote that captures the essence of each story. The scriptures are replete with stories of forgiveness. Each of you probably has your own favorite scriptural passage on forgiveness. We encourage you to recall those passages, reread them, and reflect on them, asking yourself, "Where is God drawing me?"

The final section, Part III, reminds us of the special grace that we, as Catholics, have in the sacrament of penance. In this section and two appendices, we will look at the God who loves us and how sin is a turning away from that love. We will provide an examination of conscience on forgiveness as a way to personally integrate all that you have read and reflected on. Jesus has left us a unique gift of forgiveness, the sacrament of penance. Many people have shared with us their confusion about the sacrament as it has evolved in the last few decades. Hopefully, this section will help you appreciate the healing affect of this sacrament.

The final appendix offers some practical processes for using the material in this book in a parish setting.

Our world today longs for disciples of forgiveness and disciples of hope. By choosing to become disciples of forgiveness, we not only transform our own lives but also help transform those with whom we interact. By becoming disciples of forgiveness, we evolve into disciples of hope and begin to offer options to those who live with seemingly no hope in our sometimes too violent world.

Our prayers are with you as you begin this journey.

part 1

BELIEFS ABOUT AND EXPERIENCES OF FORGIVENESS

◇◇◇

1

BELIEFS ABOUT FORGIVENESS

Before reading the vignettes of forgiveness and encountering the faces of forgiveness found in Part II, it is important to clarify your beliefs about forgiveness. This exercise should take a minimum of thirty minutes. However, you may wish to spend even more time. We share some of our beliefs as a catalyst to stimulate your own thinking. We are not asking you to evaluate our beliefs but rather to clarify your own.

Our Beliefs about Forgiveness:

- Forgiveness is a gift from God.
- Forgiveness is a gift to oneself.

- Mature forgiveness moves beyond the gift to oneself to a concern and a compassion for others.

- Forgiveness is an act of the will, a decision to let go of the desire to get even with someone who has hurt you.

- Jesus preached forgiveness, the loving of one's enemies.

- Forgiveness is the essence of what it means to be a Christian.

- There is a difference between forgiveness, reconciliation, and justice.

- We forgive because God has forgiven us.

- We forgive because we need to be healed.

- The person who chooses not to forgive is devoid of the power to love.

- Forgiveness is a slow process.

- Research indicates that forgiveness is the trait most strongly linked to happiness.

- It takes courage to forgive.

- Forgiveness is the only solution for the violence in our world today.

- Forgiveness does not have to be communicated to the other.

- Forgiveness does not imply approval of the behavior of the other.

- Forgiveness is not easy and is not the normal human reaction.

- One of the reasons why people do not forgive is that they do not have any models of forgiveness in their lives.

- Not to forgive is to be a perennial victim of those who have hurt us.

- Forgiveness will not result in forgetting.

- Forgiveness is the treatment of choice for anger.

- God sometimes gives people the grace to forgive immediately.

- We are students in the school of forgiveness. Jesus is our teacher.

- God moves our hearts to forgiveness; we cannot do this by ourselves.

My Beliefs about Forgiveness

Please take some reflection time to articulate in writing your own beliefs about forgiveness. If you keep a journal, perhaps you could record them in it. You do not have to limit yourself to any specific number of beliefs.

It's weak
They win" and forgive
I don't try to
punish them, then
they get off scott free
only stupid people forgive
they never have to pay any price
for what they have done.

must always be "RIGHT"
so they are wrong
I'm not RIGHT if I forgive

I MUST MAKE THEM PAY
wimpy NON-forgiveness
My NON-forgiveness hurts them.
If they were wrong
they need to apologize
I want them unhappy.

2
Personal Experiences of Forgiveness and Non-forgiveness

The discussion of forgiveness will not begin with the philosophy or theology of forgiveness. Rather, we begin from the premise that people learn about forgiveness primarily through the experience of forgiveness, both of forgiving and being forgiven. The most important experience of forgiveness is to experience God's forgiveness of us as sinful people in need of healing. Forgiveness is most profound when we know that God has forgiven us, when we are the recipients of God's gift of infinite mercy and love.

We assume that you have chosen to read this book because you desire to become a more forgiving person. To help with that desire, we offer you opportunities for personal reflection to increase your awareness of the experience of forgiveness. In order to make that experience personal and real, we invite you to explore some initial faces of forgiveness. These are your experiences. Later we will share the powerful stories of others who have made the decision to forgive or not forgive and the consequences of those actions.

We encourage you to make these experiences as personal as possible. In so doing, you will become more aware of the times when God has touched your life with the overwhelming gift of forgiveness.

Experiences of Forgiveness

Recall a time in your own life when you have caused pain to someone by what you have said or not said, done or not done. Using your power of visualization, place yourself in the presence of that person. Allow yourself to experience the sense of pain and regret that followed from your actions. Now visualize yourself sitting with that person. Initiate a dialogue with that person. Drawing on the strength of your own will, tell the person that you are sorry for having hurt her/him. Picture that person attentively listening to your apology. Ask for forgiveness for what you have done. In your reflection, can you hear the other say, "I accept your apology? Yes, I do forgive you. Let's let it go."

If so, what effect does that have on you? What emotions does it evoke? Can you feel the weight being lifted from your shoulders? If, on the other hand, the other person does not accept your apology and expression of forgiveness, can you accept the fact that you have done all you can do? You have acted as a person of integrity. You have initiated a process of forgiveness, but you have no control over the other person. The person either chooses to accept or reject your offer. You can only initiate the process of forgiveness. You have no control over others' response or ultimate reconciliation.

If you are not able to engage in this mental process, ask yourself, why not? What are the obstacles within you that prevent you from taking action that will bring you a greater sense of life and hope?

Experiences of Non-forgiveness

In the previous experience, the other accepted your apology and your pleas to be forgiven. However, sometimes the outcome is different. The other person refuses your request to be forgiven. Again, place yourself in a situation where you are sitting with someone you have hurt. Ask for forgiveness. However, this time the answer of the person you have offended is different. Perhaps the response is, "In time maybe, but now I cannot forgive you," or, "I will never forgive you!"

To receive such a response is extremely painful. Perhaps a couple of examples will be helpful. The first experience was a personal one. After prayer and reflection, I realized that I had indeed offended someone rather deeply. Having built up enough courage to go to the person and apologize, I was admittedly taken aback by the person's inability to forgive or even desire forgiveness. I do not stand in judgment of that person, but it is a powerful reminder that sometimes the face of forgiveness is a sad one and not one of reconciliation and acceptance.

The second example was recently shared with us by a young priest, Father Sean. He had just finished celebrating Mass, and on his way out of church he stopped to greet some of the parishioners. As he extended his hand in greeting to one of the ushers, he was taken aback when the usher, whom he barely knew, refused his handshake. His surprise and shock were compounded by the fact that they had just celebrated the Eucharist, the sacrament of unity, together. The vehemence of the usher's response shook him. He was stung by the man's response, "I have no respect for you. I do not forgive you for the way in which you have hurt me and others."

Experiences of Being Offended or Being the Forgiver

The picture on the cover of the January 8, 1984, issue of *Time* magazine is usually etched into the mind of anyone who has seen it. It shows Pope John Paul II sitting in the prison cell of Agca, the man who shot him. Agca is leaning toward the Pope, seemingly listening intently to what the Pope is saying. It is evident that they are involved in a very personal and intense dialogue. To our knowledge, the specifics of that conversation have never been revealed. I do not think that it is possible for us to know completely what took place in that conversation. *Time* magazine emphasized the general content of that dialogue. It was about forgiveness and reconciliation. Apparently, it had an effect on Agca, since years later he was quoted as saying that Rome is the place of the devil but that the Pope is a good man. Forgiveness and

reconciliation have the power to transform our perceptions as well as our relationships.

In the previous experiences we asked you to be with
and engage in conversation with someone whom you
have hurt. We now ask you to repeat the process from
above, only this time do it with someone who has hurt
you. We invite you to imitate what Pope John Paul II
modeled for each of us. Can you allow yourself to sit in
the presence of someone who has seriously offended you
and tell that person that you forgive him or her? Again, as
above, we ask you to consider the questions posed about
your desire to forgive or about the resistance you have
toward forgiving. It may help to have an objective person
who can accompany you to arrive at this decision.

Questions for Personal Reflection

As you begin this journey toward forgiveness, we
invite you to ponder two important questions. First, who
has not yet forgiven you for something that you have
done to offend them? The second question is equally
important and just as profound. In your heart is there still
someone that you have not yet forgiven? It is important
that you put a face and a name to each of these questions.
By naming who may not have forgiven you, and by naming someone you have not yet forgiven, you are invited
to participate in the sacred reality of mercy in which God
wishes to embrace us.

It is important to admit to ourselves that the realities
of being forgiven and offering forgiveness are usually

messy and often heart-wrenching. However, the antici-
pated pain and messiness does not excuse us from beginning the process of forgiveness. Ultimately, we are all
bound by the injunction of Jesus in the gospel that we
forgive as God has forgiven us. We acknowledge that it is
much easier to say, ". . . Forgive us our debts, as we also
forgive our debtors . . ." (Mt 6:12) than to do it.

It is only through God's grace that we can forgive
one another from the heart. But if we do not see this
grace offered to us, we will not know how to let God's
gift bear fruit in us. Thus, it is important to study models
of forgiveness: Jesus, the unique, divine-human model,
as well as those who try to live and forgive like him. As
Saint Paul said so well, "Take me for your model, as I
take Christ" (1 Cor 11:1).

part 2

THE FACES
OF FORGIVENESS

◇◇

3
CHRISTINE:
Beginning the Process
of Forgiveness

*"Say to Joseph: I beg you, forgive the crime
of your brothers and the wrong they did in
harming you."*

—Genesis 50:17

The most devastating and shocking incident in the lives of most Americans was the terrorist attack on 9/11. Even the mention of that infamous date continues to bring sadness, depression, and rage. Individuals who lost a loved one on that day, not surprisingly, maintain that their lives will never be the same. The devastation to life and hope are much more powerful than the visible destruction of buildings.

About two years after the attack we were conducting a parish mission retreat in New York, within sight of where the World Trade Center had once stood. On the second night of the mission Christine approached and asked to speak with us. She told us that her son, an employee at the Twin Towers, died in the fire and collapse of the buildings. His body was never recovered. Christine talked about her constant depression over the last two years. She was frozen in time. There had been no abatement of her pain. She knew that her grief, her anger and her depression were destroying her. Christine had difficulty describing what she was feeling. At times there was more emptiness than feelings.

The previous night we had discussed the topic of anger and forgiveness and invited people to consider how refusing to forgive was affecting them. We talked about how holding on to anger and resisting forgiveness could have serious implications for them, destroying the soul, the body, and the heart. Christine told us that although it was very difficult to listen to our challenge, she had spent the night crying and praying. By morning she came to the point where she could acknowledge the retreat as a special blessing from God. She honestly confronted the reality that her rage was destroying her. Christine said, "They killed my son. Now they are killing me, and I am letting it happen." Christine realized that she had a choice: to continue to internalize the anger and watch herself die slowly, or to wrest the power from the terrorists and begin the slow, difficult process of healing and forgiveness. She acknowledged how difficult it would be but she was willing to try. She did not want to be another casualty or victim of 9/11.

We stood in awe of this woman and recalled the words of Nelson Mandela, that only courageous people forgive. He had proven that. Now this distraught, courageous mother was also proving it.

Christine decided to begin the process of forgiveness. She realized that taking the first step would not be easy. It would be a long and difficult process with successes and failures along the way. The first step in the journey provided some initial relief and freedom. It helped her experience other emotions that had been suppressed and repressed. As Martin Luther King, Jr., declared, refusing to forgive prevents us from experiencing love and other emotions. Forgiveness restores life.

Questions for Personal Reflection

1. What is the most traumatic experience I have ever had in life? How has that experience affected me?

2. Will I be courageous enough to take the first step in the journey toward forgiveness?

3. What will be the most difficult part of the journey toward forgiveness for me?

4
APRIL:
Forgiveness,
a Gift to Oneself

*"Let anyone among you who is without sin
be the first to throw a stone at her."*
—John 8:7

Collaboration is based on the belief that God has
gifted people and calls them to use their gifts in
ministry. As part of our workshops on collaboration we
usually include a process for discerning gifts. In preparing
people for the process of discerning their gifts we attempt
to expand their concept of gift, emphasizing that every
experience in life, even the most painful ones, has the
potential for discovering new gifts.

While conducting the gift-discernment process as
part of a diocesan program we requested a group of
people known to each other to model the process for
the others. After explaining the procedure and stressing
the spiritual and religious nature of the experience, April
began to share her gifts. She shared that she had gifts for
organization and for radiating joy. After sharing her first

two gifts there was a silence, and we turned to see April sitting tearfully. Finally she blurted out that she also had the gift of knowing what it is like to be a fifteen-year-old unwed, pregnant teenager. Her revelation touched the lives of many in the room. Immediately after the process one woman informed April that she just received a call from a teenager in her parish who thought she might be pregnant. She asked April if she would be willing to talk with the girl. Other participants came to ask April if she would be available to talk to the teenagers in their parish. April's personal transparency, although difficult, was a grace that touched many that day.

The next day April was present at another diocesan program. She came forward to share with us how healing the experience of the previous day had been for her. April discovered that the pain, the shame, and the guilt that she had endured as a teenager, she now perceived as a gift that she could use to touch the lives of others experiencing similar circumstances.

April indicated that sharing her experience had helped her come to a deepened realization of the need to forgive herself. No one is perfect. Each of us, as Saint Paul says, does things that we wish we had not done. But we have a loving God who will, like the forgiving father in the scriptures, lavish us with his love and forgiveness. If only we were as forgiving toward ourselves as God is toward us, we would come to the fullness of our Christian life. Saint Francis de Sales preached to his followers that to get up over and over again after a fall is much more attractive to God than if we never failed at all. Mother Teresa of

Calcutta often said, "We are not called to success. We are called to faithfulness." The mature Christian is the faithful Christian, not the perfect one. Mature Christians can forgive themselves and accept God's forgiveness. God does not want us to be paralyzed by our sins of the past, but rather to accept his mercy and to forgive ourselves.

Questions for Personal Reflection

1. What are the areas in my life where I have been less than perfect? Do I experience God's call to conversion, forgiving myself and accepting God's gift of mercy?

2. What are the issues in my past life that continue to provoke shame within me?

3. What are the areas where I find it difficult to forgive myself?

5
NIGEL:
Choosing Forgiveness Over Anger, Bitterness, and Revenge

"So when you are offering your gift at the
altar, if you remember that your brother
or sister has something against you, leave
your gift there before the altar and go; first
be reconciled to your brother or sister."
—Matthew 5:23–24

On a recent visit to Pakistan, where I gave a retreat to a group of seminarians, I met a young man, Nigel, with a moving story of forgiveness and reconciliation. Nigel met me at the airport in Karachi along with two others. During our introductions I immediately noticed that he had some deep scars on one of his cheeks.

During the week of the retreat Nigel met me in the garden and said that he would like to share with me how he received the scars. He had worked one summer in a marmalade factory in his hometown. He worked on the assembly line where the glass jars were filled with marmalade. One of his supervisors, having learned that he was a Christian, became very resentful toward him. The supervisor was of another religion.

One day the supervisor approached Nigel and accused him of defiling the food being placed in the jars with his "Christian" hands. The man became so angry that he took an empty jar and crushed it on Nigel's face causing the scars.

Nigel was then fired and sent away. With time he realized that as a priest he would proclaim the gospel of Christ to others, and so he had to reconcile with this man and forgive him. He knew that he had to put into practice the words of Jesus: "If you bring your gifts to the altar and there remember that your brother has something against you, go and be reconciled and then come and offer your gifts." Nigel spoke often over the next weeks with a priest-friend who encouraged him to write the man a letter asking for reconciliation. Since it was the time of a religious holiday for the man who had been Nigel's supervisor, he also sent an appropriate greeting card.

When Nigel returned home from the seminary during Christmas break, there was a knock on the door. Nigel opened the door, and to his great surprise, the former supervisor was there with the letter Nigel had written. He asked Nigel, "Why did you write this letter?" He answered, "Because I am a Christian, and I must be reconciled with everyone; I consider every person to be a brother or sister." The supervisor, with tears in his eyes, replied: "I need to ask your forgiveness because I was the one who did wrong." Then he handed Nigel two jars of the factory's marmalade as a Christmas gift.

They spoke for a while and then embraced in a gesture of reconciliation. Before leaving, the supervisor asked the seminarian, "What will you do about the scars on your face?" Nigel replied, "Whenever I look at myself in the mirror, I will be reminded of our friendship and that we are brothers."

As I have reflected on this incredible story of forgiveness, I have come to appreciate that the young man I met could have been angry, bitter, and full of revenge. Instead, I met and have become friends with a young man who expresses joy and peace. He radiates a beautiful sense of interior freedom and love to all he meets.

Questions for Personal Reflection

1. When I look at my scars caused by others, what do I see?

2. To fully live the message of Jesus regarding forgiveness demands humility. Do I need to ask God for the gift of humility that leads to mercy?

6
JOHANNA:
Becoming Whole

*"But I say to you that listen, love your
enemies, do good to those who hate you,
bless those who curse you, pray for those who
abuse you."*

—Luke 6:27–28

Forgiveness has the power to make you whole. This is especially true when a negative action or attitude causes profound trauma in your life.

Johanna was only thirteen when, at the end of World War II, she, her mother, and other residents of Breslau, Germany, were forcibly evicted by Russian soldiers. Even today she cannot speak or write about the horrors of that death march, other than to say that she and her mother experienced beatings and rape nightly. Through the three weeks of terror, and for many months after, her mother insisted that the two of them pray a rosary every evening for their tormenters.

"I thought those rosaries were the most ludicrous things we could ever do," Johanna recounted. She would argue with her mother, asking why they had to pray for the soldiers. "Do you know of any who are more in need of prayer for their salvation than these men?" was her mother's simple answer.

Years later Johanna recounted this story to a stranger at a workshop. He became very serious. "You know of course, that those rosaries saved your life?" he said. Aside from the spiritual salvation of the prayers, he pointed out that the ability of a victim to recover is often dependent upon the ability to let go of the hatred and feelings of helplessness. "As you prayed for those who harmed you, you entered into the pain of their weakness," she remembered the stranger explaining. "They needed the prayers of you and your mother in order to attain the greatest good that anyone can hope. Your prayer reversed the roles. The victim became the one who had power. They were no longer a controlling force in your life. Finally, you no longer hated them; your life was not preoccupied with their deeds. You were free to continue living. You probably are now beginning to forgive them, and that has made or will make you whole."

Johanna, like any child, was unable to see the wisdom her mother was imparting. With the simplicity of the mind and heart of a child, she could only see that these soldiers were violating her. Her mother's exhortation to pray for those who were abusing her seemed ludicrous. Probably all Johanna could feel was the rage and desire for revenge.

Her mother, though, because of her innate wisdom and deep faith, was able to look beyond the abusers and peer into her own heart and decide what would eventually bring her wholeness. She discerned what was the best thing to do for herself, as well as what was the right thing to do.

Johanna, now in her seventies, has gradually come to realize the wisdom passed on to her by her mother. She is not an eternally powerless victim. Rather, she made the decision to be the master of her own spiritual and emotional life. Her decision has been a decision for life.

Questions for Personal Reflection

1. Am I still an emotional victim of someone who has abused or hurt me in some way in the past? Why do I allow that person to control my life?

2. Do I pray for those who have abused or hurt me? In what ways might Johanna's story help me to do that?

3. What prevents me from making the life-giving decisions in my life?

7
DEBORAH MORRIS:
Forgiveness as Personal Freedom

Have mercy on me, O God. . . .
Wash me thoroughly from my iniquity,
and cleanse me from my sin.
—Psalm 51:1–2

Many individuals are familiar with Sr. Helen Prejean, C.S.J. Her extraordinary pastoral ministry with prisoners on death row has been documented in her book *Dead Man Walking.* The book, later made into a very successful movie, has helped to bring the issue of capital punishment to the forefront of consciousness.

Less well known, perhaps, is a woman named Deborah Morris, who authored a book called *Forgiving the Dead Man Walking.* Morris was raped by Robert Willie, a key figure in Prejean's book. It was many years after Willie had died in the electric chair that Morris could finally bring herself to forgive this man who had violated her. She wrote of her personal soul-searching journey where she finally arrived at the point of forgiving. While being interviewed on the talk show circuit, she was often asked how she could possibly forgive this man who apparently never showed any remorse for his actions. Morris's response is a challenge to all Christians. Like Nelson Mandela, who declared at his inauguration as President of South Africa that if he did not forgive he would still be in prison, Morris offered similar wisdom. She declared that what she surrendered in the decision to forgive was "all her Robert Willie stuff," her shame, her guilt, her lowered self-esteem.

As already noted, forgiveness is a gift to oneself. Morris's forgiveness had no effect on Willie. He was dead. Her decision to forgive was a choice for life for herself. It meant that she would no longer be his victim. She would be free of his emotional control over her life. Not to forgive allows the person toward whom we are angry to live rent-free in our mind, heart, and soul. Forgiveness is about freedom. It is the gift of life that one gives oneself.

For too long our culture has propagated the myth that when one truly forgives, one will forget. There is nothing further from the truth. Deborah Morris will never forget what Robert Willie did to her. Christian forgiveness is all about remembering, not forgetting. The Christian is called to forgive seventy times seven. In other words, the Christian is called to recall the hurt and to continually choose to forgive. As intelligent human beings, we do not forget the pain of situations, nor do we forget the one who has caused the pain.

I remember receiving a little gift one day that had a three by five index card attached. On it was a pencil

eraser and under it was written, "God erases our sins."
Is that actually true? God forgives our sins, but to erase
something is to pretend that it never existed or that the
offense never took place. God chooses to forgive us while
acknowledging what we have done wrong. To forgive
and forget is neither a healthy nor a mature response.
What is truly healthy and holy is to begin by acknowledging the reality of what has happened. Then, with God's
help and compassion, we may choose over and over to
forgive those who have sinned against us.

Questions for Personal Reflection

1. Whom do I allow to have control over me because I
   withhold forgiveness?

2. Have I been indoctrinated with the myth of "forgive
   and forget?" If so, do I experience guilt when I continue to remember the terrible things that were done
   to me?

8
ANN LANDERS:
Letting Go of the Past

*"I will remember their sins and their
lawless deeds no more." Where there is
forgiveness of these, there is no longer any
offering for sin.*
—Hebrews 10:17–18

One of our favorite authors on forgiveness is the late columnist Ann Landers. In her column she frequently included letters of lives that had been transformed through the acceptance of the simple advice to forgive and release the accumulated self-inflicted pain that results from holding on to anger. She counseled her readers to do themselves a favor and make the decision to forgive someone who had offended them. Her advice was consistently simple and direct. She reminded those who wrote to her that choosing not to forgive was, as the author Louis Smedes notes, a decision to suffer. Landers was so convinced of the power and need for forgiveness that she lobbied for a National Day of Forgiveness. Many of her readers responded to this invitation, as evidenced by the countless letters she would receive from people whose lives had been transformed by initiating the process of forgiveness. The letters spoke of the freedom and new life they experienced in choosing to seek out those from whom they had been alienated.

Our favorite Ann Landers column on forgiveness was a letter she received from an older woman. The woman shared how fifty years ago her husband had had an affair. When the writer discovered her husband's infidelity she confronted him. Fortunately they were able to be reconciled. But to indicate the emotional depth of this affair, the husband informed his wife that the other woman had loved him so deeply that she had promised that she would commit suicide if he ever left her. To drive the point home even more forcefully, he then, in a rather passive-aggressive manner, informed his wife that if the other woman did commit suicide, it would be the wife's fault!

The writer went on to describe what transpired recently. Fifty years after the incident she decided to call the "other woman" to inform her that she had forgiven her. To her surprise and dismay she discovered that the other woman did not recognize her, barely remembered her husband, and, in fact, probably did not remember him at all.

The wife declared that she "could kick [her]self" when she thought of the heartache she had gone through for fifty years while the other woman had totally forgotten the situation.

Forgiveness is a gift to oneself. People provide all sorts of rationalizations for holding on to their anger. Often it has to do with inflicting pain on the one who has hurt them. In the end, though, they are forced to admit that anger destroys their life and happiness. When this reality is accepted they are in a position to begin the process of forgiveness.

Questions for Personal Reflection

1. Is there someone from whom I have been long alienated because I have chosen to hold on to my anger for months, years, or decades?

2. Do I see forgiveness as a gift to myself?

3. Have I had any experiences where choosing to forgive replenished life for me?

9
MORRIE:
Forgiveness of Self

"Have you sinned, my child? Do so no more, but ask forgiveness for your past sins."

—Sirach 21:1

Tuesdays with Morrie is a powerful, insightful, and moving book. The author, Mitch Albom, discovered that one of his university professors, Morrie Schwartz, was dying from a degenerative illness of the muscles. Morrie had had a profound influence on Mitch's life. As often happens when one ventures from school into the world of work, Mitch had lost contact with Morrie.

Mitch had become a newspaper writer in a town distant from Morrie's home. Upon learning of Morrie's illness Mitch immediately made a decision to visit Morrie. This led to weekly visits each Tuesday. He wanted to convey his appreciation to Morrie and realized that he still had much to learn from Morrie's wisdom. This book, which became a bestseller and movie, is filled with the wisdom that Mitch gleaned from Morrie on those sacred Tuesdays.

Among the many poignant moments in the book is one related to forgiveness, specifically forgiveness of self. Mitch quotes Morrie saying, "Forgive yourself before you die, then forgive others. . . . There is no point in keeping vengeance or stubbornness. . . ."

Morrie had been reminiscing about a very close friend of his named Norman. When Morrie's wife, Charlotte, had a serious operation, Norman had failed to contact Morrie. As a result, Morrie became exceedingly angry with Norman. Morrie recalled how he had withheld his forgiveness even though Norman had tried several times to become reconciled. Now, Morrie, lying in his bed and crying as Mitch rubbed lotion into his "lifeless toes," mourned his stupidity. He quietly sobbed, "I never got to forgive. It pains me now so much." Morrie concluded by telling Mitch, "It's not just other people we need to forgive. We also need to forgive ourselves."

While the lack of adequate models is the major obstacle to forgiveness, a second major obstacle is the failure to forgive oneself. Although we are convinced of the infinite love and forgiveness of God, too many Christians fail to act Christ-like toward themselves. Peter van Breemen claims "The sacrament of reconciliation is complete only when we forgive ourselves."

In no way do we wish to imply that forgiveness of self is an easy process. To move toward self-forgiveness is extremely difficult and usually requires the assistance of a caring, sensitive other. There appears to be an internal mechanism in most healthy people that arouses a fear that one is being too easy on oneself when there is a movement toward self-forgiveness.

Forgiveness is a central tenet of the New Testament. Why is it that so many of Christ's followers have such a difficult time forgiving themselves? Perhaps the lack of self-forgiveness is a repetition of the original sin of pride in the Garden of Eden.

Questions for Personal Reflection

1. Have I forgiven myself for those acts that are contrary to my own values?

2. What prevents me from forgiving myself?

3. Who are my models for forgiveness?

10
NANCY AND FRANKIE:
Forgiveness, a Decision for Personal Healing

"And forgive us our debts, as we also have forgiven our debtors."
—Matthew 6:12

We present workshops on many different topics, but inevitably, the topic of forgiveness generates the most questions and discussion. Forgiveness seems to touch a universal chord in the hearts of people. There is an innate hunger and desire to discover ways to let go of the intolerable pain and suffering that result from the inability to forgive.

During the Jubilee Year of 2000 we were invited by a diocese to speak on the themes of that year, one of which was forgiveness and reconciliation. On the second day of the workshop a participant from the previous night came forward. She handed us a playbill from a play her daughter had recently been in and pointed to the director's dedication, saying that it spoke of forgiveness. We read that the play was dedicated to two individuals, Nancy and

Frankie. The director had written that Nancy, his sister, had recently been attacked and brutally stabbed until, as he described, "the kitchen floor was flooded with her blood." Immediately after the murder, the killer, Frankie, drove away and committed suicide.

The director wrote of his personal struggle with the tragedy. He was filled with a complexity of emotions. He spoke of the hatred that overwhelmed him and his family. That hatred was intermingled with the confusion and sorrow that they all experienced.

In the midst of these intense emotions the director decided to attend the funeral of his sister's murderer. He told his family of the decision, and they reacted with confusion, annoyance, and anger. Their reaction challenged him to reflect on his decision and the reasons for it. After reflection he knew that it was the right thing to do. The decision had no rational basis. He concluded that the response could have come only from God's intervention. His decision challenged the entire family to examine their own responses. In the end, the whole family came to the same decision and attended the funeral of Nancy's murderer.

The family sat together and "mourned the death of a killer's life." The director recounted kissing Frankie's mother and asking God's blessing on her. At that moment the family, not surprisingly, "felt God's peace." "God changed our family," the director wrote. He described the transformation that occurred within his family as a result of their choice to forgive. Forgiveness is a decision, an act of the will. Forgiveness is not an emotion. It is a choice to let go of the desire for revenge or to harm someone who has caused us pain.

The change that this family experienced relates to the promise Jesus gives to us in the Our Father. Jesus has made it very clear: we will experience God's love, mercy, and forgiveness to the degree that we choose to let go of our anger and to forgive." *The Catechism of the Catholic Church* reminds us that God's peace, love, and mercy "cannot penetrate our hearts as long as we have not forgiven," (*CCC*, 2840). The family had the courage to forgive, and so they felt God's forgiveness, peace, love, and mercy. As Mahatma Gandhi has taught, "Forgiveness is a virtue of the brave."

Questions for Personal Reflection

1. How does the director's story affect me?

2. Do I have the courage to forgive those who have harmed me in some way?

3. Are there times when I feel devoid of God's peace? Could this be related to my unwillingness to forgive others as God forgives me?

11
SISTER JANE:
Forgiveness, a Human Need

> *"Blessed are the merciful: for they will*
> *receive mercy."*
> —Matthew 5:7

A number of years ago an article in *Time* magazine focused on the pope's forgiveness of his would-be assassin, Mehmet Ali Agca, and indicated that, "forgiveness runs somewhat against human nature." The article reminded us of the oft-quoted adage of Alexander Pope: "To err is human and to forgive divine." Perhaps there is need to question this statement because forgiveness is at the essence of what it means to be truly human.

Two religious women shared stories about one of their sisters, Sister Jane, who suffered from Alzheimer's disease. The stories show us that forgiveness is a human need.

Sister Jane became very angry, as is often the case for Alzheimer's patients, toward Sr. Marguerite, who was assisting her with her daily needs. The incident occurred just prior to the communal liturgy. Immediately after the liturgy Sister Jane went to her religious superior and stated that she had become upset with and hostile toward Sister Marguerite. The two had been good friends and lived together for years, but Sister Jane could not recall Sister Marguerite's name. Sister Jane, who was experiencing daily diminishment and who could not even find her own bedroom without assistance, humbly confessed to the superior how she had become angry and attacked "some sister." A woman whose vocabulary had become more and more restricted and whose ability to master simple daily tasks had been severely diminished announced, "I need to become reconciled with her." Even in her dementia, Sister Jane acknowledged her human need for reconciliation.

This story indicates the pervasive human need for forgiveness and reconciliation. Although Sister Jane's mental faculties were diminished, she realized the need for forgiveness and reconciliation at the very core of her being. Forgiveness is initiated by God who has placed this desire in our hearts.

Another of Sister Jane's community members, Sister Victoria, shared an additional story about a conflict between the two women decades before the onset of Sister Jane's Alzheimer's. Soon after the conflict Sister Jane approached Sister Victoria and invited her to go to a movie. Before they had even begun to talk about the possibility of reconciliation, Sister Jane had begun the process of forgiveness and was able to extend herself to Sister Victoria. Because of Sister Jane's maturity in initiating the reconciliation, the two sisters were able to bridge the chasm that separated them and become reconciled. For Sister Jane forgiveness and reconciliation were values that were so intense that even in her dementia she was compelled to take the initiative to begin the process of healing.

Questions for Personal Reflection

1. Are there significant people in my life from whom I have become alienated? Is there a need and desire for forgiveness and reconciliation?

2. Have I encountered someone like Sister Jane who easily initiated the process of healing when there had been disruption in a relationship? How grateful am I for that person?

3. Is there healing that I need to initiate? Am I willing to take the first step?

12

ROBERT ENRIGHT:
Forgiveness and Reconciliation

*All this is from God, who reconciled us to
himself through Christ, and has given us
the ministry of reconciliation.*
—2 Corinthians 5:18

At least three state universities' psychology depart-
ments have conducted research on the topic of forgiveness. The University of Wisconsin has become most
prominent for its research in this field. The lead research-
er, Robert Enright, has been quoted extensively when
incidents of violence appear in the media. Enright and his
colleagues did extensive research on young women who
were sexually abused as children. In the process of this
research they were confronted with the rage and hostility
that these helpless victims, now adult women, felt toward
those individuals, often trusted family members, who had
perpetrated these atrocities.

In the course of their research Enright and his colleagues came to appreciate that the anger, rage, and
hostility experienced by these women, though perfectly

understandable, was destroying them. Because these women unintentionally gave power to their perpetrators, they continued to be victimized by them. They were women frozen in the tragic event of the past. In time they realized that they had complete control over whether or not this continued abuse would cease. The researchers realized that the treatment of choice to heal the open wounds was to forgive.

In working with the women the researchers faced a common misconception. The misconception is that forgiveness must involve verbal communication with the offender. The researchers advised the women that they need not communicate forgiveness to their abusers. They also strongly discouraged any communication with their assailants if such action would put the women in a position of potential harm and vulnerability. Instead, they helped the women to discern the difference between forgiveness and reconciliation. Forgiveness is an act of the will, a choice, a movement of the heart, and there is no obligation to communicate this, unless one wants to achieve reconciliation with the other. In the case of some of these women, reconciliation would put them into a potentially perilous situation. However, in other cases, when reconciliation was desired and seen to be indicated for the healing process, then an attempt at reconciliation was recommended.

Too often the belief that forgiveness must be communicated to the other and that reconciliation is always a desirable condition, prevents individuals from considering forgiveness.

Questions for Personal Reflection

1. Can I distinguish between forgiveness and reconciliation?

2. Do I hold the myth that for forgiveness to be complete, it must be communicated to the other? If so, how does this affect me?

3. Do I perceive forgiveness as a movement of the heart that involves God rather than just an act of the will?

13
RICHARD:
Forgiveness, a Curative Factor

"I came that [you] may have life, and have it abundantly."
—John 10:10

A newspaper recently ran an article citing the story of forgiveness and reconciliation between people of two different cultures who had perceived each other as mortal enemies.

Richard had been a young soldier who fought with the United States troops in Vietnam. He had become obsessed with hatred for all Vietnamese people. His hatred stemmed from watching close friends being killed during the war. The hatred he felt was an intense, palpable sensation that was constantly with him. The emotion was so deep that it began to eat away at his very being, leading to a life-threatening ulcer and ultimately the need for an operation.

While recovering in the hospital after the operation, his doctor informed him, "I can fix your stomach, but I can't cure your head." Richard suddenly awoke to what he was doing to himself. He recalled crying like a baby when he realized how self-destructive he had been. In recent years the connection between health and forgiveness has begun to be examined more closely. It is not uncommon now to find programs in hospitals with titles like this one: "Spirituality and Healing in Medicine: The Importance of Forgiveness."

Holding on to anger and hatred can kill you spiritually, physically—as in the case of Richard—and emotionally. Constant anger produces too much ACTH which is cortisol, metacortisol, and adrenaline. Too much of those enzymes released continually into your body can cause a life-threatening ulcer such as Richard had developed. It can also produce many other physiological reactions, such as heart attacks and strokes.

Fortunately, this story had a happy ending. The newspaper included a picture of Richard meeting with a neighbor who was a Vietnamese soldier during the time when Richard was in Vietnam. Richard had met the Vietnamese soldier, Tran, at a church meeting. Richard, reflecting on the words of his doctor, experienced a conversion of heart, and realized that his own health and happiness depended on his decision to let go of the anger and forgive.

"What Makes People Happy? Psychologists Now Know: It's Not Great Riches, But Friends and Forgiveness" was the title of an article that appeared in *USA Today*. The article quoted University of Michigan psychologist Christopher Peterson, who said, "Forgiveness is the trait most strongly linked to happiness." As we have repeated numerous times, forgiveness is a gift to oneself. It assures that we will be both happy and healthy.

The article relating Richard's story emphasized that Richard had not only arrived at a point of forgiveness, but also, through his relationship with Tran, had achieved reconciliation. When forgiveness leads to reconciliation, it is an extraordinary gift. However, reconciliation is not always possible. If the other person does not choose to become reconciled, we are helpless to force it. We have complete control over forgiveness. We choose to forgive or we choose to hold on to our anger and destroy ourselves. But, we must remember that we do not have the power individually to bring about reconciliation. This is something we can only offer.

Questions for Personal Reflection

1. Do I have anger and hatred that is destroying me?
2. Do I have physical ailments that might be attributed to anger?
3. How will I remind myself in the future that forgiveness is mine to choose and reconciliation requires the participation of the other?

14
MARTY JENKO:
Forgiveness, the Heart of Love

"Father, forgive them; for they do not know what they are doing."
—Luke 23:34

Over the course of a lifetime we encounter many individuals, saints and sinners alike. Joseph Campbell claims that "mystics and madmen swim in the same waters. One drowns and the other is reborn." We were privileged to meet one of those mystical saints who made the decision to convert a personal hell into an experience of being reborn. He was Father Marty Jenco, a Servite priest. We met Marty when he was a participant in a workshop for campus ministers. Before serving as a campus minister, Marty Jenko had been held captive in Beirut, Lebanon, for nineteen months.

Marty's life had been dedicated to ministering to the poor and alienated. It was this dedication that brought him to Lebanon to work with the Catholic Relief Services. Marty described his experience of being held hostage. He later published the full story as *Bound to Forgive:*

The Pilgrimage to Reconciliation of a Beirut Hostage. His central message throughout the book was, "Jesus taught us that the heart of love is forgiveness."

There is one unforgettable, poignant incident that Marty shared with us and is captured in his book. It is the story of one of his captors, Sayeed, a man who had often brutalized him. Marty watched a change take place in Sayeed. Initially Sayeed called him by his last name, then by his first name, Martin, and finally *Abouna,* an Arabic name meaning "dear father." Marty noticed that along with the change of name to a more personal one, there was a corresponding change in the tone of voice, indicating that a change of heart was taking place. Finally, Sayeed sat on a mat next to a blindfolded Marty and asked if he recalled the first six months of his captivity. Marty responded, "Yes, Sayeed. I remember all the pain and suffering you caused me and my brothers." At this point Sayeed asked, "*Abouna,* do you forgive me?"

Marty grappled with his response. It was neither immediate nor automatic. He knew at a cognitive level that he was called to forgive. Yet he struggled with the decision to forgive and to let go of his desire for revenge, retaliation, and vindictiveness. Finally, he reluctantly came to the realization that he had to forgive. His deeply ingrained Christian values compelled him to do so.

We too grapple with forgiving another. We find strength in Jesus who asked his heavenly Father to forgive those who had brutalized him.

Questions for Personal Reflection

1. Who are the individuals who have persecuted me? Am I willing to overcome my desire for revenge and restitution to begin the process of forgiveness?

2. Am I able to be patient and compassionate with myself as I struggle with making the decision to forgive?

3. Are there times when I have persecuted others? How did they respond?

15
MARIE AND BILL:
Forgiveness and Spousal Relationships

"For this reason a man will leave his father and mother and be joined to his wife, and the two will become one flesh."
—Ephesians 5:31

Forgiveness, we have learned, is necessary to healthy relationships. In marriage, it is even more essential for couples to forgive, "seven times seventy," in order to be faithful to their sacramental commitment "for better, for worse . . . until death do us part." Couples can mistake their willingness to put aside a divisive issue and go on with their lives as a sign of forgiveness. A bouquet of flowers, the preparation of a special meal, or an unexpected night out can signal either a request for forgiveness or the acceptance of repentance by either spouse. If, however, the hurt is never talked about and the ongoing dialogue does not allow both to feel as if they have been heard, then the buried hurt only hibernates for yet another season. Then, when a new hurt erupts between them, it re-emerges even stronger. When such a pattern persists, couples may reach the limit of what they are willing to forgive, and the relationship is often irreconcilable.

Infidelity can be one of those failures that crosses the line of many peoples' ability to forgive. Married couples who prepare other couples for marriage often raise this concern: Couples about to be married put limits on their willingness to forgive. Pastoral ministers struggle with this attitude of selective forgiveness and wonder if the engaged couples are setting themselves up for a failed marriage. What does "for better or for worse" mean to them? If there are limits on a partner's willingness to forgive the other, are they able to make such a commitment? In this period of discussion, a woman whose husband had died recently shared this story.

Marie and Bill attended their own marriage preparation prior to their wedding. Particularly after the talk on the sacramental aspect of marriage, Marie knew she wanted to be completely honest with Bill about her relationships prior to their engagement. She felt that her omission was a lack of honesty and could be an obstacle in their marriage. Her way to mend this was to ask forgiveness for her lack of openness and honesty. After telling Bill her story, she could see by his expression that it was having a profound effect on him. Marie's intimacy with another had shattered Bill's dream of being the first and only man his wife would ever love. For the first time in their relationship, a moral issue stood between them. Marie does not know all that went through Bill's head and heart when he heard the story, but she is sure he was hurt, disappointed, and confused. She told us how deeply his words touched her and how they had a profound effect on her spiritual life and their future marriage. With tears in her eyes, she shared what she remembered he said to her.

His question was simple: "Have you talked with your confessor about this?" He said to her that if she had gone to confession, then he knew that God had forgiven and so would he. Marie was aware that the people in the group may have had differences of opinion about the appropriateness of Bill's question. This, however, was irrelevant to her. For Marie, only one thing mattered. She was loved so deeply that Bill was willing to let go of his personal hopes and expectations. His belief in the sacrament of penance was a gift to both of them. Marie also shared with the group that this was the first time they had been so open and honest with each other. She knew, beyond any shadow of doubt, that she was marrying a man who believed in forgiveness. "Our marriage," she said, "began on the premise that anything and everything can be forgiven." She also told the group that the covenant they shared on their wedding day was based on the belief that God would always be with them. The sacrament of penance provided each of them with a place to go where they could honestly reveal their most naked self and receive the forgiveness that is an integral part of their relationship with each other, and with God and the Church.

Questions for Personal Reflection

1. Do I have a list of commissions or omissions that would be unforgivable? Do I know why this is?

2. It is suggested that within relationships we can be challenged to become the best of who we are meant to be. If I enter into a committed relationship with limits to my forgiveness, can it still be called "committed"?

3. If forgiveness is not an option for me, then what is my best option?

16
J.R.R. TOLKIEN:
Forgiveness, Restoring Right Relationships

> *"A new heart I will give you, and a new spirit I will put within you; and I will remove from your body the heart of stone and give you a heart of flesh."*
> —Ezekiel 36:26

Anger is a powerful, intense emotion. When it is misdirected or used negatively anger can cause harm to individuals, families, and even to the entire world. Forgiveness, on the other hand, has the power to transform these same relationships. Pope John Paul II preached that "Forgiveness is the only way to peace between peoples and nations." Dag Hammarskjold, former Secretary General of the United Nations, wrote in his diary during Easter of 1961, "Forgiveness breaks the chain of causality."

Peter van Breemen, in *The God Who Won't Let Go*, expands upon this conviction of Dag Hammarskjold and writes that anger and hatred result in a vicious, satanic, ever-expanding cycle. Van Breemen states that, "Hatred causes and justifies violence, and violence, in turn, stirs up hatred." He believes that the only way to break this vicious cycle is through forgiveness. Van Breemen declares that without forgiveness, our world "is losing its human face and the reflection of its Creator."

This vicious cycle can probably be seen most clearly at the level of the family. Each of us is probably aware of families that have been torn asunder and destroyed by the decision to withhold forgiveness.

A brief article appeared in a newspaper recounting the story of the family of J.R.R. Tolkien, the author of *The Lord of the Rings*. The article described the deep division that occurred in the family over the decision to make *The Lord of the Rings* into a movie. Simon, a grandson of the author, supported the movie's production. His seventy-seven-year-old father vehemently opposed the decision. As a result of their differences the father would have nothing to do with Simon, nor with Simon's eleven-year-old son.

As we reflected on the article we were struck with pangs of sadness. Because Simon's father was unable to let go of his anger, he had become alienated from both his son and grandson. The elder Tolkein's inability to forgive and seek reconciliation with his son must have left a permanent void in his own life.

The greater sadness, though, is that this story is not an isolated example. In our ministries we encounter too many families who have condemned themselves to isolation and loneliness because they have not had the courage to forgive. Nelson Mandela once said, "courageous people do not fear forgiving." Too often personal pride becomes the stumbling block to peace and harmony at both the family and world level. Holding on to anger precludes our ability to love. Martin Luther King, Jr., said that the person "who is devoid of the power of forgiveness is devoid of the power to love."

Questions for Personal Reflection

1. Are there members of my own family from whom I am alienated? If so, am I willing to take the first step toward forgiveness?

2. What stands in my way of mending the brokenness of relationships?

3. Can I invite God into these relationships of alienation and desire his way of peace?

17
MARY:
Looking into the Eyes of the Persecutor

"He will wipe every tear from their eyes.
Death will be no more; mourning and
crying and pain will be no more."
—Revelation 21:4

Mary was returning home. For most people, home-comings are often filled with deep emotions, some-times conflicting ones. For Mary, who was a refugee, this homecoming was particularly poignant. Since she was forced to leave her homeland twenty years earlier, much had happened. She was the only surviving member of her family; all others had perished either resisting a brutal dictatorship or in the flight from their burnt-out city.

Although the departing occupation forces were still monitoring the streets, she had decided it was impor-tant to see if her childhood home was still standing. She ventured across the border with friends and walked with them through the city, mourning lost landmarks and changed landscapes. Finally, one friend took her by the arm. "Mary, we're not doing this anymore," he said.

"Doing what?" she asked.

"Avoiding the soldiers," he replied. She was completely unaware that, as they had walked the sidewalks, she would go into the streets to avoid passing the soldiers on the sidewalk. She had thought that in twenty years, she had worked through the hatred and fear that she once had of that drab uniform, but apparently not. "You are going to walk right up to these men and look them directly in the eyes," her friend said, taking her gently but firmly by the arm.

She felt her heart beating wildly as they walked up to a group of uniformed men. And then she looked into their young eyes.

"At that moment I realized that I could not hate anyone," she said. These were not the men who drove her away from her homeland, who killed her family and made her a penniless refugee. And even those who had hurt her, she realized, were themselves misled. While Mary could hate injustice, cruelty, even her memories of torture, she could not hate a human being. Eyes are windows into the soul. Those young soldiers' eyes reminded Mary that everyone—no matter what their actions or sins—is created to be one with God. And who can hate that?

Too often we allow those who have hurt us in the past to influence how we perceive people in the present. Mary viewed the soldiers she encountered in the present through the eyes of her tormenters of the past. It was her ability to look into the eyes of the people she was encountering in the present that brought her to the realization that she was incapable of hatred.

In *The Wounded Healer,* Henri Nouwen shared the tale of a village that gave sanctuary to a young fugitive. When the soldiers discovered that the fugitive was hiding in the village they gave the villagers an ultimatum: hand the fugitive over, or the entire village would be massacred. Unsure what to do, the villagers approached the rabbi and asked his advice. The rabbi began praying for wisdom. As he read the scriptures his eyes fell on the passage, "It is better that one man dies than that the whole people be lost." He saw this as a clear sign from God and informed the villagers to tell the soldiers where the fugitive was hiding. The next night an angel appeared to the rabbi and told him that he had handed over the messiah to the soldiers. The rabbi was crestfallen and defensive, and asked the angel how he could have known. The angel replied, "If instead of reading the scripture, you had visited this young man just once and looked into his eyes, you would have known."

Questions for Personal Reflection

1. Have I ever looked into the eyes of someone I hate? Have I allowed myself to look beyond those eyes into the soul of the other? If so, how did it change my heart?

2. How fearful am I to look into the one who has offended me? What am I afraid of discovering about myself?

18
JUDY AND BOB:
Forgiveness and Justice

O Lord our God, you answered them;
you were a forgiving God to them,
but an avenger of their wrongdoings.
                                    —Psalm 99:8

Forgiveness is normally a slow process. Usually when there is an attempt to rush to forgiveness it results in pseudo-forgiveness. There are times, however, when God grants a spontaneous gift of forgiveness. When this occurs, it must be acknowledged as a special gift from God.

While conducting a workshop on forgiveness we asked the participants, a group of deacons and their wives, to identify someone who had witnessed for them what it means to forgive. Everyone turned toward one couple sitting in the corner. Asked why the response was so instant and universal, the husband, Bob, began to slowly and solemnly recount their story. Bob and Judy's twenty-five-year-old daughter, Christine, was kidnapped, raped, and murdered. Earlier in her life she had been in an auto accident resulting in an extremely long rehabilitation process. Just days before she was murdered, Christine had called her mother to relate excitedly that she was beginning to regain her short-term memory. There was great joy in the family. Their joy would be short-lived.

Eventually the police captured the murderer who was one of their neighbors. The man was brought to trial and eventually convicted. Although Bob and Judy's friends all believed that the killer should have received the death penalty, the couple did not agree. Their response to their friends was that to take the killer's life would have been "a desecration of the sacredness of Chris's life." Christine loved life and loved people.

Bob and Judy have forgiven the man who murdered their daughter, and it is their ardent hope that God has also forgiven him.

However, the couple was aware that the murderer was a man who was prone to violence. There were prior episodes of violence. On several occasions his wife was hospitalized as a result of his severe beatings. They became aware of numerous other incidents when he acted violently toward others in the neighborhood. Although Bob and Judy forgave Christine's murderer, they also pleaded with the judge not to release this criminal into society. The couple was convinced that if the murderer were released, his violent nature would probably lead him to rape or murder again.

Bob and Judy had the ability to distinguish between forgiveness and justice. If this distinction is overlooked, it can become an obstacle to forgiveness. Forgiveness does not dissipate the obligation for justice. Pope John Paul II, who forgave Ali Agca, the man who attempted to assassinate him, developed the intricate connection between peace, justice, and forgiveness in his message delivered at the celebration of the World Day of Peace on January 1, 2002. Relating his own personal experience with both Nazi and Communist totalitarianism, he declared that, "Justice and forgiveness are both essential to . . . healing." In that message he provided one of the most beautiful definitions of forgiveness when he said, "Forgiveness is above all a personal choice, a decision of the heart to go against the natural instinct to pay back evil with evil."

Several years ago terrorists murdered some members of a religious community. We listened to the surviving members of the community struggling to make a choice to forgive. Their struggle came from the realization that the murderers, having shown no remorse, were likely to murder others if they were released. Initially, the community failed to make the necessary distinction between forgiveness and justice. Forgiveness does not take away the responsibility of justice. Once they were able to make this distinction, the community members were able to forgive.

The struggle between justice and forgiveness is sometimes apparent among the divorced, particularly when physical or emotional abuse has been present in the relationship. The abused party may believe forgiveness removes the accountability for the abuser's acts of violence. Forgiveness and justice, while not incompatible, are separate issues.

Questions for Personal Reflection

1. Are there limits to my forgiveness? Are there certain situations that would make it impossible for me to forgive?

2. If I or someone close to me were murdered, would I be able to forgive the murderer? Would I request that the murderer not be given a death sentence?

3. When was the last time that I prayed for the gift of forgiveness?

19
A BISHOP:
A Simple Act of Forgiveness

For the Lord is compassionate and
merciful;
he forgives sins and saves in time of
distress.

—Sirach 2:11

Forgiveness is not always a dramatic action. Sometimes the most transforming examples of forgiveness are extremely simple.

While working in a diocese we were invited to stay at the home of the local bishop. It was a quiet Sunday and the bishop had already had a full day performing his episcopal duties. As we relaxed he excused himself saying that he had a meeting with a woman who was a former employee of one of the diocesan institutions. As she was leaving the bishop's home at the conclusion of the meeting, we heard her exclaim, "Reconciliation is a wonderful thing!"

Later we heard the full story. The bishop has a reputation as a very pastoral and compassionate man. However, like every leader, he was often required to make difficult decisions.

He approved the dismissal of the woman with whom he had just spoken. Her immediate supervisor had recommended that she be fired, and the bishop approved the supervisor's recommendation without further investigation. Later, when he learned of the pain caused by his decision, he contacted the woman and expressed his apologies and sorrow over any pain that he may have caused. The bishop then asked if they could meet so that there might be some further dialogue and possible reconciliation. The meeting that Sunday was the result of the invitation. The woman's comment at the conclusion of the meeting and the light banter that followed indicated that reconciliation had taken place.

True reconciliation often leads to new understandings about oneself. In addition to being pastoral and compassionate, the bishop was also wise, humble, reflective, and insightful. He shared what he had learned from the experience. As he had reflected and prayed about his actions, the bishop came to the realization that he had handled the situation poorly. Due to pressures and time constraints, he had taken "the easy way out." He had accepted the word of the supervisor without offering the woman who was to be fired an opportunity to share her perceptions of the situation. He realized that his behavior had cost him the trust and respect of the woman. He had gone against his principle of always talking directly with people. When he realized the pain his decision had caused, he called to apologize and to offer the opportunity to meet and seek reconciliation. She was deeply touched by the bishop's initiative and accepted the invitation. However, due to a number of circumstances, it was two years before they could finally come together and be reconciled.

This vignette is a simple example of reconciliation, yet there is much to be learned from it. South Africa, after Apartheid, established the Truth and Reconciliation Commission. Drawing from this model, the first step for the bishop was to acknowledge the truth of his actions. Because of his maturity, he was able not only to acknowledge his mistakes, but also to initiate a process of reconciliation. This can be a difficult decision because one is never sure of what the other person's reaction will be. The next step in this process is to initiate a face-to-face encounter that allows for honest, and often difficult, dialogue. Although this process can be extremely painful, the results, as seen from this vignette, can be transforming for both parties. For the woman, there was a sense of peace and the transforming experience of reconciliation. For the bishop there were new understandings about himself and a renewed commitment to follow his own principles.

Questions for Personal Reflection

1. Is there someone with whom I need to become reconciled? Am I willing to take the initiative to begin this process?

2. Have I had the experience of initiating dialogue that led to reconciliation? What did I learn about myself in the process?

3. Are there times when I am challenged to look at my own actions that have caused pain to others? Have I made amends with that person?

20
LUC AND ROBERT:
Attitudes and Their Effect on Forgiveness

"But I say to you that if you are angry
with a brother or sister, you will be liable
to judgment; and if you insult a brother
or sister, you will be liable to the council."
—Matthew 5:22

There are many obstacles to forgiveness. One such obstacle is the attitude that we have toward the person we wish to forgive. Attitudes give shape to the mental image we have of others. When we maintain negative images of another, forgiveness toward that person becomes difficult. We are like projectionists in a theater. We choose the pictures and images that play on the screen of our minds and hearts, and only we have control over the images that we place on that screen.

Luc shared his personal story of how changing his image created the potential for forgiveness. As a cradle-Catholic the words of the Our Father were ingrained in him: "Forgive us our trespasses as we forgive those who trespass against us." His parents reinforced this by their direct injunctions, "Tell your brother you're sorry." "Shake hands and go play." These injunctions provided formative components that he carried with him into his adult life. In his adult years he finally understood the full impact of the words of the Our Father and embraced its message.

Until 1998 Luc and his wife Diana had lived a charmed life. The trouble that seemed to impact other families had not affected them. This immunity collapsed when his brother-in-law, Robert, killed his own wife. Robert called it euthanasia because she was terminally ill. Luc and Diana labeled it murder. Robert was convicted and is still in prison.

The killing had occurred while Luc was two thousand miles away on a business trip, and he felt a mixture of guilt, helplessness, and anger. His helplessness led him to prayer. Prayer began the healing process for him, not in an immediate, miraculous way, but gradually. He still experienced anger toward his brother-in-law. He was not yet ready to forgive him. Luc had a strong desire to punish Robert for what he had done to the family, but Robert frequently contacted him and asked him to visit him in prison. Luc's anger was so intense that he refused to see Robert. Gradually, Luc came to the realization that retaining his anger was hurting him—physically, emotionally, and spiritually—more than it was hurting Robert. He realized that the anger was poisoning him.

Finally, Luc went to visit Robert. As he looked into Robert's tearful eyes and heard his plaintive cries for forgiveness, he finally relented. He saw the presence of Jesus in Robert. Luc's attitude began to change, and he could see the love and compassion that had motivated Robert. When Luc realized the anger and judgment he had harbored toward Robert, he begged Robert for forgiveness. They embraced and cried together. Luc knew that they had reached a point of mutual respect. Although he is still not reconciled with Robert's actions, he no longer holds resentment. He feels as though a heavy burden has been lifted from him. Once he was able to understand Robert in a new way, his attitude toward Robert changed, and forgiveness was not only possible, but almost compelling.

Luc summarizes it this way, "Both Robert and I have learned the value of forgiveness. The gift we received in that moment of forgiveness and reconciliation allows each of us to continue on our spiritual journey with a clearer mind knowing that the love and compassion of our savior Jesus Christ is alive and well in both our hearts."

The words of the Our Father now have new meaning to Luc. He has made them his own.

Questions for Personal Reflection

1. Can I think of someone toward whom I harbor resentment? Can I identify the attitude I have toward this person?

2. Can I see the picture I continue to run in my mind that determines these attitudes?

3. Am I willing to begin the process of changing my attitudes?

21
TOM AND LOIS:
Parents as Models of Forgiveness

*"But while he was still far off, his father
saw him and was filled with compassion;
he ran and put his arms around him and
kissed him."*

—Luke 15:20

Daytime-television watchers are inundated with talk shows that tend to glorify stories of "dysfunctional families." Daily they are invited to be voyeurs, peering into the secret depravity of families. Adult children deplore their upbringing, raining condemnation on their parents, blaming them for having traumatized them. These programs tend to portray these aberrations as the norm. Tired of being bombarded by these stories from the media wasteland, many long to hear the good news stories of normal Christian families. We have been privy to many such stories. The two we will share highlight parents who modeled forgiveness in such a way that it has transformed the lives of their children. Remember that the first school of forgiveness is the life of Jesus. We

learn to forgive by being drawn into his life and by experiencing his mercy and compassion. Next, we learn from
others, especially our families.

The first story was recounted when we asked students
and faculty at a seminary to identify the person who
had witnessed forgiveness for them. Without hesitating
one of the faculty members, Tom, shared how his father
was the major witness in his life. He recounted a specific recurring incident from his youth. When Tom was
a pre-adolescent boy his father went to confession every
week. Tom shared how every Saturday before leaving for
church, his father would come to him and ask his forgiveness for whatever he had done the previous week to
offend Tom. Needless to say, this act of mature humility
made a permanent impression on Tom's life. The actions
of his father provided Tom with an understanding of
forgiveness and the sacrament of penance that influenced
his entire life.

A second story was related by Lois, who after a session
on the topic of forgiveness at a parish mission shared a
family story. Lois related that her brother, Bill, had been
in a very serious accident. As a result he had numerous
operations and lived with constant pain for years. His
mother, a wise woman, observed that Bill not only was
suffering from physical pain, but also from emotional
pain. One day, in a typical maternal way, she sat down
with Bill and with great compassion, advised him to forgive the man responsible for the accident. She, like many
mothers, was able to see beyond the surface to the depth
of his soul. After some initial reluctance Bill finally made
the decision to forgive. Lois told us that he not only

began to experience an emotional healing and a sense of peace, but there was also even an almost miraculous healing of his leg.

Both these stories attest to the potential that parents have to influence their children. Sometimes they do it through words and sometimes through actions. As Pope Paul VI taught, "People don't listen to teachers [or parents], they listen to witnesses." Both these parents witnessed the value of forgiveness for their children. In both cases it changed the lives of the children. The children adopted the values of their parents. As Saint Francis of Assisi is reputed to have said, "Preach the gospel and sometimes use words." Children learn to forgive or not forgive primarily from the witness of their parents. This mother and father serve as models for all parents.

Questions for Personal Reflection

1. How have I been a witness of forgiveness to my children, my students, or any youth that I have potential to influence?

2. Even if my parents were not "perfect," can I accept the concept of "good enough" mothering or fathering and learn from their positive qualities?

22

BISHOP WILLIE WALSH:
Forgiveness and Sexual Abuse

> *After he had washed their feet, had put*
> *on his robe, and had returned to the table,*
> *he said to them, Do you know what I have*
> *done to you? You call me Teacher and*
> *Lord—and you are right, for that is what*
> *I am. So if I, your Lord and Teacher, have*
> *washed your feet, you also ought to wash*
> *one another's feet.*
>
> —John 12:12–14

Every so often in life we are fortunate enough to encounter people who, through the way they live their lives, leave an indelible impression on our mind, heart, and soul. Bishop Willie is such a person, a source of edification. He creates such a welcoming and warm climate that people spontaneously want to confide to him what is most important in their hearts and souls.

Some priests from his diocese shared with us an incident that is characteristic of Bishop Willie. One of the priests of the diocese had been erroneously accused of sexual abuse. During the Sunday liturgy at which the falsely accused was re-installed, Bishop Willie stopped in the middle of his homily, set aside his prepared text, and said to the congregation, "How difficult it is to be a priest today." At that point he began to cry, and a young teenage girl emerged from the congregation with a tissue in hand to dry his tears. He is one of the most human and compassionate bishops we have had the privilege to meet.

Bishop Willie modeled a unique way of attempting to concretely foster reconciliation in the wake of the sexual abuse scandal. In December 1999—in preparation for the new millennium—he made a "Pilgrimage of Reconciliation" across the diocese in an attempt to begin a process of reconciliation and healing, and to beg pardon not only for the sins of sexual abuse committed by those acting in the name of God and of the Church, but also for all the hurts that people had experienced in and from the Church and its leaders.

His journey lasted three weeks and wound its way through forty towns and villages. Bishop Willie, who was in his mid-sixties at the time of this pilgrimage, walked from church to church in the diocese in the cold, rainy December weather. He took no umbrella and simply carried a plain wooden pastoral staff, the symbol of his role as shepherd. The members of the parish where he had just presided over a healing and reconciliation liturgy would accompany him half way to the next parish, where he would be met by members of the parish where he was next going. They would then begin the journey of penance with him to their parish. When he arrived at the parish he would celebrate the reconciliation service.

The pilgrimage was an attempt to help anyone who had suffered any type of abuse from any member of the Church. The invitation to join in the pilgrimage was intended for everybody. They would not only walk with him, but they would take advantage of the opportunity to talk with him. The priests of the diocese shared many stories they had heard from those who had joined him and whose lives had been helped by their encounter with him. They spoke of the healing they experienced as they would leave the crowd following him and approach to speak privately with him. Some of those who joined him later recounted that it was the first time in their life they had shared the memory of abuse with another human being. Others recounted how they had personally experienced the healing touch of God and the tenderness of the Church in their experience of walking and talking with this humble man. Still others described the experience in a more profound way. They compared it to the journey to Emmaus described in the scriptures. They had truly walked with God.

What began as a simple journey concluded in transforming the lives of many who had been victims of abuse and brought some healing to the entire diocesan church which was experiencing great pain. Pope John Paul II, in his encyclical *Mission of the Redeemer,* declared that there were two gestures that characterized Jesus in scripture, healing and forgiveness. This pilgrimage of reconciliation accomplished healing and forgiveness for many.

Questions for Personal Reflection

1. Who has witnessed forgiveness and reconciliation for me in the way that Bishop Willie did for the people of his diocese?

2. Which Church leader has modelled Jesus for me in the way he or she responded to the sexual abuse in the Church?

3. How does Bishop Willie's action challenge me personally?

23

CATHERINE:
The Ebb and Flow of Forgiveness

*He sees and recognizes that their end
is miserable; therefore he grants them
forgiveness all the more.*

—Sirach 18:12

We have established that forgiveness is a decision reached through a slow and often painful process. It requires patience. The feelings associated with forgiveness come and go; they do not remain fixed. It can be confusing to reach the decision to forgive and then periodically experience anger and resentment. The circumstances and the person being forgiven play a part in the recurrence of ambivalent and angry feelings. The more complicated the circumstances, the more complex the forgiveness process.

Sitting in a McDonald's restaurant one day watching her children play, Catherine revealed to her mother that when she was a child, she had been molested. Catherine then informed her mother that the molester was her brother. The older woman, obviously shaken and undoubtedly not wanting to face the fact that her son could do such a horrible thing to his sister replied, "Oh my God." Then she turned her head and never mentioned the revelation again. Feeling rebuffed, Catherine buried her long-held secret even deeper and distanced herself from the family both geographically and emotionally.

Ten years later at a family party Catherine's older sister, Anita, witnessed an inappropriate incident involving the same brother and one of her young male cousins. Not sure what to do, she mentioned it to her father and mother. The mother glared at Anita and walked away. Anita, perplexed by her parents' response, telephoned Catherine and related the story. During the conversation Catherine revealed her molestation by this same brother.

Family chaos ensued. A large, close family fractured and moved apart. Relationships were broken. Anita, assuming the family would want to resolve the problem, unsuccessfully attempted to bring the family together with a professional counselor to sort out the situation. In her attempts to arrive at some resolution she felt stonewalled at every turn. Over a period of time the molestation became a secondary issue. An inordinate amount of hostility was directed toward Anita. She was accused of breaking up the family when all she sought was honest and open discussion.

Catherine and Anita's mother made it very clear to her daughters that her primary interest was maintaining relationship with all of her five children, and that meant not calling her errant son to accountability for fear the relationship with the other children would suffer. The errant son appeared to be protected by the family, and the two sisters were left to deal with the pain of the molestation and family break-up on their own.

The story is complicated by the fact that the elderly mother's brother was a priest who over the years had become somewhat the family patriarch. The revelation of the molestation within the family coincided with the clergy abuse scandal in the Catholic Church and seemed to follow the same course. The priest's solution was to call everyone to forgiveness quickly and move on with life. His intentions, while good, did not allow for the fact that forgiveness is a lengthy and slow process and that this serious problem called for help beyond what the family could offer each other.

Five years later the family still suffers. The parents remain adamant in protecting the family secret; the siblings are alienated. The brothers have coalesced, forming a group, while the two sisters are ostracized. To this day the family has never discussed the incident or the effects it has had on all of them.

The sisters periodically discuss the levels of forgiveness they have each achieved, the therapy they have each pursued, and the prayers they continue to offer. The process is difficult and ongoing.

A tentative level of reconciliation has taken place within the family. However, because the issue was never addressed directly, anger, hostility, and frustration surface regularly when the family is together.

The mother described in this vignette attempted to deal with a family crisis by ignoring it. Like many of us, she believed that ignoring the issue would maintain peace and unity in the family. The opposite is true. The failure to address the issue honestly and openly has prevented any real forgiveness or reconciliation from occurring. Like the proverbial elephant in the living room, they live constantly with the "secret" infecting all their family dynamics.

Questions for Personal Reflection

1. How have the dynamics in my family fostered or hindered forgiveness and reconciliation?
2. Have I been a victim of sexual abuse? How have I dealt with it? What more needs to occur?
3. Can I chart the ebb and flow of forgiveness in my life?

24
CINDY:
Forgiveness as an Act of Faith

You forgave the iniquity of your people;
you pardoned all their sin.
You withdrew all your wrath; you turned
from your hot anger.
                                    —Psalm 85:2–3

Cindy Broaddus was a victim of a random act of violence. Several years ago, she and her friend Jim were
leaving Oklahoma City for a vacation. Early in the morning, as they drove under an overpass on the outskirts
of town, someone dropped a canister of sulfuric acid
directly onto their car. It took but seconds for the acid to
eat its way through the windshield and to cover Cindy's
body with burns that not only threatened her life then
and there, but have impacted her every day since. Late
one evening, I watched Cindy being interviewed on the
Larry King Live show. Her story had just been published
in a book entitled *A Random Act*. As she shared her
extraordinary story, I was impressed with several turning
points in particular that determined the outcome of this

horrific act. She described her recovery as a miracle of love, faith, and forgiveness.

Early into the interview, she spoke of a faith that would not allow her to feel sorry for herself. When asked if she ever asked God, "Why me?" her answer was, "I never once asked 'Why me?' Never. I don't believe in that. If I ask 'Why me?' it's almost like I'm saying I didn't deserve this and someone else does." How willing are we to take this thoughtful reflection into our own faith experience? How many day-to-day events are we tempted to take personally rather than see them as a consequence of the human choice for evil? This non-personal response can offer us many opportunities for reflection and discussion within our own faith communities.

At another point in the interview, Cindy also spoke of forgiveness as a personal choice. When asked if she forgave the person who did this to her, her answer was an unequivocal yes. She said she totally forgave the perpetrator. Again she said, "I feel like forgiveness is a gift I give myself. You know, I could let this turn me bitter and that would only affect me and mine. It's not affecting him and his. So there was no reason not to forgive him, and I have forgiven him." Her response about forgiveness ended there. She did not seem to need to prove her case and have us agree with her. She knew what she had to do to continue her recovery and that was all that mattered to her.

The interview covered a variety of life issues, but mostly she talked about the ability to make choices: choices that impact each of us in our everyday lives;

choices to forgive and to decide what kind of survivors we are going to be; choices about the values that direct our lives when they are so drastically changed that there's little left of what came before the tragedy. Cindy Broaddus believes her greatest choice came in her decision not to be hurt over and over again by going through life as a bitter and angry woman. She chose instead to be grateful for waking up each day to share life with her children, grandchildren, family, and friends.

Questions for Personal Reflection

1. What is the most traumatic, negative experience I have had in life? Have I forgiven the person who was responsible for that trauma? If not, why not?

2. In what specific ways does Cindy Broaddus witness faith to me?

3. What values direct my life? Do I allow negative experiences to make me a bitter and angry person?

25
KATHY:
Forgiving God

Job said to God, "Why should I be a target
for you? I waste away . . . let me alone"
                                    —Job 7:12, 16

Many people, who have grown in their ability to express anger toward people in their lives, still find it extremely difficulty to express that same anger toward God. There is a strongly entrenched injunction, developed from their earliest formation, which proclaims that anger toward God is bad, evil, and sinful. Some would remind us, after all, that anger is one of the seven capital sins. However, a rereading of the *Catechism of the Catholic Church* indicates that anger is no longer listed as one of the seven capital sins. It has been replaced in that list by wrath. Anger is an emotion. Wrath is a behavior used to express that emotion, a behavior that attacks the other as an enemy. Nevertheless, many Christians still harbor the belief that a good Christian should never become angry, and certainly should never, under any circumstances, become angry with God.

A friend of ours, Kathy, has somehow managed to escape this terrible fear of becoming angry with God. Her life has been characterized by a series of debilitating illnesses and escalating pain. Each time that she learns to cope with one condition, she is diagnosed with another. It was during a period of particular pain and frustration that we talked with Kathy. We were overwhelmed by the vehemence of her anger toward God. She sounded like a character from the Old Testament, railing at God with a flurry of invectives.

Interestingly, it is exactly because Kathy can allow herself to feel and express her anger toward God that she has such a personal, intimate relationship with God. It is akin to what happens in any human relationship. If I cannot allow myself to get angry with someone, I may not be able to feel love toward that person.

A psychiatrist we know proposes what he calls the "single channel theory." Picture a conduit running through your body, similar to the veins and arteries that carry blood throughout the body. Sometimes those vessels become blocked with plaque and the blood is unable to flow through the body. "The single channel theory" however, refers to a conduit that carries, not blood, but emotions. Of course there is no such tangible channel in the human body. But, perhaps, our psychiatrist friend theorizes, our emotional conduit sometimes becomes blocked as a result of not acknowledging and accepting certain emotions. This blocked channel then makes it impossible to feel other emotions such as love.

Recently we heard Kathy talk about how she eventually forgives God after having been angry with him. Her favorite cousin, who has been an emotional support to her, recently died. Kathy told us that after she stormed against the Lord, she gradually came to the point of deciding to forgive God. It was not a quick process. She continued to do battle with the Lord, but then, fully believing in God's goodness, she was moved to forgive God.

People sometimes ask, "Why should we forgive God? God is perfect love and compassion and would never do anything to hurt anyone. Perhaps a human example might help. Have you ever acted lovingly toward a person only to have that person interpret your loving action in a negative way and experience severe anger and pain as a result? Sometimes we interpret God's actions as hurtful, even though God was acting lovingly.

Mature people allow themselves a broad range of emotions in any relationship. Why should it be different with God? Try, like Kathy, to allow yourself to experience and express your anger toward God.

Questions for Personal Reflection

1. Am I aware of times in my life when I have been angry toward God? Why? How did it feel?

2. Am I intimate enough with God to argue with him?

3. When I feel angry with God, do I stop talking to him or do I continue to express my true feelings toward him?

26
MARGUERITE:
Forgiveness and Creative Response

When Mary came where Jesus was and saw him, she knelt at his feet and said to him, "Lord, if you had been here, my brother would not have died." When Jesus saw her weeping . . . he was greatly disturbed in spirit and deeply moved. . . . Jesus began to weep.

—John 11:32–35

We can think of no greater tragedy for a parent than the suicide of a son or daughter. Our travels to various places have exposed us to heart-wrenching stories of parents who are struggling to live with the pain and confusion of a suicide. Suicide is always difficult to accept, and parents are often almost inconsolable. They are overwhelmed by loss, grief, and anger, and experience myriad other emotions too complex to untangle.

This is one woman's story. Marguerite's teenage daughter, Alice, had committed suicide over ten years ago. Marguerite discovered her daughter's lifeless body asphyxiated by carbon monoxide from a car that had been intentionally left running in the garage. The doors and windows had been carefully sealed with rags and clothing. Lying next to the body was a note from Alice asking her parents to forgive her. She gave no reason for taking her life.

Marguerite was, of course, devastated. Ten years after the incident, she was still trying to sort out her reactions and emotions. She talked about her shock, her guilt, her anger, her grief, and an assortment of other, harder-to-define emotions. Initially she felt intense anger toward herself. And for no discernable reason, she experienced an equal amount of anger, rage, and fury toward her husband. Eventually, Marguerite was able to acknowledge the rage and hostility she felt toward her daughter.

For ten years, she struggled to find an answer as to why her daughter had taken her life. There was no rational reason; it was an unexplainable act. Marguerite slowly came to the realization that she would never know the reason or understand the act. She decided that she had to find a constructive way to deal with something that seemed irrational. At the point of our meeting she described herself as unwilling to live with the constant thoughts of what she should have or could have done. Eventually, through couples' counseling, she realized that neither she nor her husband was to blame. Slowly, Marguerite began to experience a peace that she had not known since her daughter's death. She indicated that time did not heal the pain; it only made it easier to live with it.

Marguerite is now able to acknowledge the anger she still feels toward her daughter. Her anger is mixed with her maternal compassion for the pain that must have enveloped her. The compassion ultimately moved Marguerite to forgiving Alice for causing such pain to her and the rest of the family.

She sought ways to deal constructively with her anger. She and her husband started a support group for other parents in the community who had also lost a child to suicide. In addition the couple decided to share their experience by publishing a book for parents of children who had committed suicide. While the book was meant to help others deal with a similar tragedy, it also helped Marguerite to verbalize her feelings and sorrow.

Marguerite's journey of ten years took her from shock, rage, and confusion to the beginning of acceptance, to a decision to reach out to others, to finally discovering a creative form of catharsis; to ultimately forgiveness.

Questions for Personal Reflection

1. Have there been events or situations in my life that seem to have no explainable reason? Can I name and still feel the pain and hurt? Where or toward whom have I directed the anger that comes from these situations?

2. Have I discovered more positive ways to deal with my anger, grief, and hostility?

27
SAMANTHA:
Guilt

"But so that you may know that the Son of Man has authority on earth to forgive sins"—he then said to the paralytic, "Stand up, take your bed and go to your home."

—Matthew 9:6

Samantha enjoyed her job and gave of herself to it wholeheartedly. In many ways, her work had become her life. While Samantha admired her coworker Helen for her gifts, she became jealous of Helen's insights and creativity. Jealousy became competition, and competition became hatred. Samantha began to use every possible opportunity to speak critically about Helen, to coworkers, family, and friends alike. At times Samantha realized that she had become obsessed with this hatred and jealousy.

After more than three years of this dreadful, tension-filled relationship, Samantha became aware of a deep-seated guilt that existed within her because of her attitude, words, and actions toward Helen. This guilt led her to realize, "I am killing Helen by what I am saying about her to others. I am also affecting our work environment. And this hatred is killing me and my spirit." Her guilt led her to deep feelings of shame and embarrassment. It moved her to talk about this relationship with a priest in confession.

Samantha calls it a miracle that she was able to go to Helen and apologize. Over a period of three months true reconciliation took place. It gave new life to their workplace, as well as to Samantha and Helen's relationship.

It would be nice if the story ended there. However, about a year later, Samantha began to relive the whole experience of hatred and jealousy. She found it hard to get it out of her mind. She began feeling guilty all over again, and the guilt became heavier and heavier. Once again, through pastoral counseling, she faced the reality of the guilt and questioned whether she had truly forgiven herself and asked whether she had accepted God's mercy.

Healthy guilt reminds us that we have done what is not "of God." This gnawing feeling of shame and regret leads us to reconciliation and healing. Unhealthy guilt, on the other hand, keeps the forgiven sin alive and nudges God's loving mercy to a second or third place. It does not allow us to begin anew, celebrate new life, or accept God's mercy as a true gift. In a spirit of healing, God invites us to be more concerned with our future than our past sins.

This story calls us to accept healthy guilt as a call to conversion and forgiveness. Unhealthy guilt is never beneficial, spiritually or emotionally. We need to invite God into our unhealthy guilt and allow God to speak these words: "You are forgiven. Go in peace."

Questions for Personal Reflection

1. When I experience guilt, do I see it as a positive call to healing and forgiveness?

2. Have I experienced unhealthy guilt? If so, how can I let it go and invite God to help me experience a healing of memories?

3. Can I truly forgive myself and accept the gift of God's mercy?

part 3

THE SACRAMENT OF PENANCE AND RECONCILIATION

◇◇◇◇◇◇◇◇◇◇◇◇◇◇◇◇◇◇◇◇◇◇◇◇◇◇◇◇◇◇◇◇◇◇◇◇◇◇

28
Sin and Forgiveness

One of God's greatest gifts to his people is his forgiveness through the sacrament of penance. In this sacrament we have God's loving guarantee of the reality, "Your sins are forgiven!" These comforting, consoling, and reassuring words are spoken by the priest who represents the merciful Christ. They assure us that God has forgiven our unfaithfulness, our sins. We experience this miracle in our own lives.

Before reflecting on this sacrament of healing, we want to ask a more basic question: "What is sin?" To discuss this question, we must ponder more deeply:

- the God who loves us and invites us to share in his life,

- our personal choice to reject God's love, which is our sinfulness,

- our understanding of sin and forgiveness.

The God Who Loves Us

We believe that we need forgiveness because we have sinned against God and others. We can only understand sin and the need for the sacrament of penance if we first know the God who loves us unconditionally and invites us to respond to that love relationship.

Our God is a loving God. He loves each of us individually. The United States Conference of Catholic Bishops document *Stewardship: A Disciple's Response* speaks of God's personal love and call to each person: "Jesus calls us, as his disciples, to a new way of life. . . . But Jesus does not call us as nameless people in a faceless crowd. He calls us individually by name." Our all-loving God has not only called us individually by name, but he has formed us in our mother's womb, has breathed his own life and spirit into us and remains united to us at every moment of our lives, calling us to a deeper personal, intimate, life-giving relationship with him. God has a dream, a hope, and a destiny for each of us. His dream is that we will recognize his love, accept it, desire it even more deeply, and continually respond to it. As Saint John tells us in his writings to the early Christians, "It is not so much that we have loved God, but that God has loved us" (1 John 4:10).

When we choose not to respond in love to God, we sin. But God does not give up on us; he offers to heal our infidelity and our sin. In the sacrament of penance, Christ the healer touches our brokenness. Gently, lovingly, and compassionately, he wraps his arms around us and speaks his word of mercy.

When we experience God's love, mercy, and forgiveness, it empowers us to share that same mercy and forgiveness with others. We can become the living, loving, forgiving presence of God to others.

In the previous section we encountered the faces of forgiveness in many different people. However, the greatest and most unique face of forgiveness is the face of Jesus Christ. In encountering the face of Christ we come to the overwhelming realization that in spite of our infidelity and sinfulness we can be reconciled to the Father and share the new life that Jesus has come to bring us.

Sin

Only when we understand the fullness of God's love for each of us can we begin to comprehend sin. Sin is not about a thing that is done or not done, a word spoken or not spoken, or a mark on the soul. It is about a broken relationship with a God who loves each of us tenderly and completely and wants only the best for us. God, in his infinite love, has given us a free will. We can accept or reject God's love in our daily lives.

Very often, we are accustomed to developing a list of sins based on our actions. Equally important are those experiences of caring we have avoided and those times when we have failed to act in a loving way. It is not only what we have done, but often what we have failed to do that causes a lack of openness to God's love and can be hurtful to others.

The *Catechism of the Catholic Church* is replete with pastoral wisdom and a holistic understanding of our faith in the area of sin. Too frequently, present culture tends to diminish the importance of sin. Karl Menninger, the famous and insightful psychiatrist, was so touched by this phenomenon that he wrote the classic book, *Whatever Became of Sin?* Our culture dissuades us from focusing on sin. We are offered many "excuses" for why we hurt ourselves and others, ranging from genetic predispositions to emotional manipulations to an excessive focus on taking care of ourselves. While all of this may be partially true, without an acceptance of our own sinfulness, there is no reason to seek God's forgiveness.

The wonderful language of the *Catechism* invites us to reflect on our own appreciation of the role of sin in our journey toward forgiveness and wholeness. We encourage you to read and reflect on paragraphs 1846 to 1869 in the Catechism and to mine the richness that is present within those insights. We will review and highlight some of those insights regarding sin with the realization that sin is a choice to close our hearts in some way to the fullness of God's love. It is that choice which convinces us of the need for the sacrament.

Sin affects and can destroy our relationship with God and with other human beings. Sin is an act of self-centeredness, a choice of people and things over God. Sin "turns our hearts away from God and true charity." It disrupts the divine plan for unity, "That all may be one" (Jn 17:21 quoted in *CCC*, 1849).

There are many different ways in which we turn away from God's love and his desire for us to care for one another. Scripture provides several lists of sins. The letter to the Galatians contrasts the works of the flesh with the fruit of the spirit. "Now the works of the flesh are obvious: immorality, impurity, licentiousness, idolatry, sorcery, hatred, rivalry, jealousy, outbursts of fury, acts of selfishness, dissensions, factions, occasions of envy, drinking bouts, orgies, and the like" (Gal 5:19–21). Matthew provides another list of sin, "For from the heart come evil thoughts, murder, adultery, unchastity, theft, false witness, blasphemy. These are what defile a person . . ." (Mt 15:19–20).

Sin is an act of narcissism. It focuses on self rather than on God and others. It is a failure to acknowledge, value, and respond to God's intimate and unconditional love. The Church reminds us that sins should be examined according to their seriousness.

Mortal sin destroys charity in our hearts by a grave violation of God's law. It turns one away from God who is our ultimate end, and from his goodness when we prefer an inferior good to him (*CCC*, 1855). Therefore, mortal sin is a personal choice to follow a false god and the values of that god; in so doing we opt for death in our relationship with God and the faith community.

Mortal sin requires three elements:

- The object must be grave matter as specified particularly in the Ten Commandments, the two Great Commandments of Jesus, the Beatitudes, and the teachings of the Church.

- It is committed with full knowledge, implying that the sinner realizes the sinful character of the act and its opposition to God's love.

- It requires deliberate consent, indicating that this is a personal choice.

The Church acknowledges that "unintentional ignorance can diminish or even remove the imputability of a grave offense" (*CCC*, 1860), as can passion, external pressures, or pathological disorders. Still, by virtue of being human, the principle of God's call to goodness is engraved in our conscience.

By contrast, "Venial sin allows charity to subsist even though it offends and wounds it" (*CCC*, 1855). Venial sin, while less grave and humanly reparable, has negative consequences. It impedes our ability to grow in our relationship with God and with one another. Venial sin is choosing to embrace evil. Nevertheless, at the core of our being, our relationship with God and the faith community is still alive, though sinful and imperfect.

While sin abounds, God's mercy abounds more. God's mercy and forgiveness are always available to us.

29
GOD'S GIFT TO US:
The Sacrament of Forgiveness

Hopefully, as we come to the conclusion of this book, you have come to the realization that within the Catholic Church, we have a unique and awesome divine gift, the sacrament of penance. You have journeyed through the vignettes of forgiveness and reflected on where and how God is calling you. Hopefully, you have discerned that God's invitation is to take advantage of this great gift.

The Church assures us that in celebrating the sacrament of penance, we not only experience God's pardon and peace, but are also reconciled with the ones whom we have wounded by our sins (*CCC*, 1422).

This sacrament is sometimes called by a number of names: the sacrament of penance, the sacrament of conversion, the sacrament of confession, the sacrament of reconciliation, and the sacrament of healing. It is a sacrament in which the priest, in God's name, makes present the forgiving Christ and his reconciliation. In the intimacy of that sacramental relationship you are free to share my most personal, shameful thoughts, acts, and attitudes that not only affected you but those with whom you share life.

The sacrament of penance makes present the forgiving Christ and it actualizes what it signifies—Christ the healer, his mercy and compassion. In so doing, we invite Jesus to enter into our brokenness, and as we receive healing, we are also reconciled with the church, whom we have affected by our weakness.

Only God can forgive sin. Jesus, the Son of God, says of himself, "The Son of Man has authority on earth to forgive sins" (Lk 5:24) and exercise this divine power: his loving response to our admission of sinfulness is, "Your sins are forgiven" (Lk 5:20). Christ delegates that sublime power to priests in the sacrament of penance. For the mature Christian who desires to experience God's forgiveness, mercy, and compassion in a very tangible way, we would hope that regular confession would be the norm, and not simply an Advent and Lenten exercise. In this way we can come to know the forgiving Christ who is at work in our lives and constantly calling us into the fullness of his life and love.

Through this sacrament God offers:

- an experience of intimacy with the forgiving God,
- greater insight into God's way of goodness,
- God's forgiveness to touch the messiness of our lives,
- reconciliation with the Church whom we have hurt.

The Sacrament of Penance

In celebrating the sacrament of penance, it is important to keep at the forefront of our minds that it is truly a sacrament of healing whereby the healing Christ touches the core of our being, giving us new life. In this sacrament it is not God who accuses us, but we accuse ourselves and realize that we are called to a change of heart and to ongoing conversion throughout our lives.

In the sacrament of penance:

- We admit that we have been unfaithful and sinned.
- We recognize our failure.
- We acknowledge that our infidelity has affected our relationship with God and others.
- We desire forgiveness and reconciliation.
- God forgives and reunites us with himself and the Church.
- New life is breathed into us.
- We are reminded that we are never to be paralyzed by sin.

Conversion continues and calls us to a change of mind and heart that we may become more like Jesus.

Rite for Reconciliation of Individual Penitents

There is still much confusion among many Catholics about "how to go to confession." The Rite for Reconciliation of Individual Penitents, included as appendix B, provides a clear model. In reading this section we would recommend that you read the rite in its entirety.

The rite allows for confession to be celebrated either behind a screen for complete anonymity or face to face in order that there might be a more informal discussion with the confessor.

The penitent enters the penitential room aware of his or her sinfulness. The penitent is greeted warmly and with kindness by the priest. The penitent then makes the sign of the cross.

The penitent may choose to read a particular passage from the sacred scriptures that proclaims God's mercy and the call to conversion. The priest may also take the initiative to read or say from memory a text from the scriptures that tells of God's mercy.

The penitent then names the ways in which he or she has not responded to God's love and expresses sorrow for sin. The Church teaches that confession to a priest is an essential part of the sacrament of penance. Mortal sins must be recounted in confession. Confession of everyday faults—venial sins—is strongly recommended by the Church. Indeed, regular confession of our venial sins helps us to form our conscience and fight against evil tendencies because it enables us to be healed by Christ and mature in the life of the spirit. Regular celebration of the sacrament enables us to experience God's mercy, and in so doing we are spurred to be merciful as he is merciful.

After the penitent confesses his or her sins, the priest proposes an act of penance which should take into account the penitent's personal situation. It must correspond as far as possible with the gravity and nature of the sins committed. It can consist of prayer, an offering, works of mercy, service of neighbor, voluntary self-denial, sacrifices, and above all the patient acceptance of the cross we must bear.

The penance that we accept from the priest is three-fold. It is an opportunity to make up for our sinful words, actions, and attitudes to "make right the wrong," for example, restoring the reputation of someone whom we may have hurt or performing works of charity and alms-giving in order to bring justice to the situation. Second, it is an opportunity to express to God our gratitude for the new life and healing that he has given to us and to celebrate that new life. Third, the penance can be seen somewhat as a medicine, a remedy, or a therapy, not only to celebrate new life, but to show us a new way to live and to embrace in a deeper way God's love and healing power.

In the sacrament of penance we are asked to name specifically those ways in which our words, our actions, and our attitudes have affected our relationships with God and others. Equally important is to look at those and ask important questions: What is the root of my sin or infidelity to God? What attitude exists in me that allows me to act or to speak in this way? What attitude or action causes me not to respond more lovingly and openly? Why do I avoid caring for others? Who or what are the false gods in my life?

The sacrament of penance calls us to a spirit of humility whereby we surrender all of our brokenness to a loving and faithful God. Jesus the healer touches our hearts, breathes new life, and calls us to conversion.

As part of the rite the penitent is given the opportunity to express sorrow, or as commonly called, an act of contrition. There are appropriate acts of contrition that many have learned in religious education. We can also formulate our own prayer that comes from the depths of our hearts, asking for God's forgiveness and for reconciliation with the Church.

Then the priest absolves the penitent in the name of Christ. The words of absolution are powerful indeed:

> *God, the Father of mercies,*
> *through the death and resurrection of his*
> *Son*
> *has reconciled the world to himself*
> *and sent the Holy Spirit among us*
> *for the forgiveness of sins;*
> *through the ministry of the Church*
> *may God give you pardon and peace,*
> *and I absolve you from your sins*
> *in the name of the Father, and of the Son,* ✝
> *and of the Holy Spirit.*

The rite of penance may end simply with an informal dismissal, or the priest may use one of the formulae suggested in the rite.

"When the priest celebrates the sacrament of penance with a penitent the priest is fulfilling the ministry of the

Good Shepherd who seeks the lost sheep, or the Good
Samaritan who binds up wounds, or the father who awaits
the prodigal son and welcomes him upon his return, and
of the just and impartial judge whose judgment is both
just and merciful. The priest is a sign and the instrument
of God's merciful love for the sinner" (*CCC*, 1465).

The Church reminds us that the confessor is not the
master of God's forgiveness, but its servant. The minister
of the sacrament should unite himself to the charity of
Christ. The priest should pray and do penance for his
penitents. The Church requires that every priest who
hears confessions is bound under very severe penalties to
keep absolute secrecy regarding the sins that his penitents
have confessed to him in the sacrament.

Review of Life

Sometimes people ask how we can adequately review
our lives. There are many forms of examination of conscience. A review of life holds up standards given to us by
Christ and the Church. Following is one model.

God and Me
- Am I open to God's love?

- Do I spend time in prayer (conversation) with God?

- Do I allow God to shepherd my life? Do I trust God?

- Do I accept God's forgiveness?

- Am I trying to see God in the events of the day?

- Do I participate in Mass on Sunday and appreciate
  being nourished by God's word and the eucharist?

Self

- Do I see myself as worthwhile?
- Do I take care of myself?
- Do I recognize and use my gifts (stewardship)?
- Am I honest with myself and others?

Family (Vocation)

- Does my family have the rightful place in my life (time, priority)?
- Do I avoid problems instead of addressing them?
- Do I respect others (spouse, parents, children, grandchildren, family, coworkers, neighbors)?
- Do I listen to others?
- Do I give and accept love?
- Does my vocation (marriage, single, clergy, religious) help to bring good to others?
- Do I honestly work at my vocation in life? Have I been faithful to my vows?

Others, Job, Society

- Do I affirm others and point out their gifts?
- Do I work towards justice, peace, and forgiveness in my daily dealings with others?
- Do I defend and protect the sacred gift of human life?
- Does my conversation build or destroy others?
- Have others become my god?
- Does pettiness and unhealthy competition exist in my life?
- Do I judge others and put them down?

- Do I use my life to help others, to love them, to bring Christ to them?

- Am I aware of the unrest, war, injustice, and poverty that plague our world? Have I done anything to alleviate this darkness?

- Am I honest with others?

We have also developed an examination of conscience that can be used to ascertain your personal growth as a forgiving person. This is found in appendix A.

We began our discussion by painting the many faces of forgiveness. The most powerful face of forgiveness is the face of Jesus Christ, which shows the radical forgiveness and love of God. By asking for and accepting the gift of forgiveness, we become more able to recognize our own faults and to ask forgiveness from God and others. We become more able to recognize when others ask for our forgiveness and the duty to forgive them.

We need to continue to paint pictures of forgiveness that have many faces. In those pictures, we must also see our own face as one forgiven and as one who seeks to forgive.

APPENDICES

APPENDIX A:
An Examination of Conscience on Forgiveness

The following questions can help guide us on the journey to forgiveness:

- Do I really want to begin the process of forgiveness?
- Why do I want to do this?
- Do I really want to become a more forgiving person?
- Who can I ask to assist me in this process?
- Am I at times an angry, bitter, or cynical person? If so, what is the hurt that is causing those destructive attitudes?
- Do I allow myself to live constantly in a negative disposition that paralyzes me and further alienates others from me?
- Do my actions reflect an attitude of forgiveness or revenge, reconciliation or violence, compassion or hate?
- What face of forgiveness is the most difficult one for me to accept?
- Since forgiveness is a gift to oneself, why do I refuse to forgive myself?
- What is my image of God? Do I experience God as loving, compassionate, and forgiving to me?
- Do I allow God's compassion, mercy, and forgiveness to touch my heart?

- Will I allow myself to be healed?

- In my heart is there still someone whom I have not yet forgiven?

- Can I allow myself to sit in the presence of someone who has seriously offended me and tell that person that I forgive him or her?

- Why do I refuse forgiveness to certain people? What is holding me back?

- Who has not yet forgiven me for something that I have done to offend them?

- Whom have I sinned against, and from whom do I need to ask for forgiveness?

- Can I accept forgiveness from others?

- What more can I do to be a model of forgiveness?

- How am I being called to be a witness of forgiveness, especially to the young people in our world today?

- In what specific ways do I witness that I truly value forgiveness, reconciliation, and compassion, the gospel values of Jesus?

APPENDIX B:
Rite for Reconciliation of Individual Penitents

Reception of the Penitent

When the penitent comes to confess his sins, the priest welcomes him warmly and greets him with kindness.

Then the penitent makes the sign of the cross which the priest may make also.

In the name of the Father, and of the Son, and of the Holy Spirit. Amen.

The priest invites the penitent to have trust in God, in these or similar words:

May God, who has enlightened every heart,
help you to know your sins
and trust in his mercy.

The penitent answers:

Amen.

Other forms of reception of the penitent may be chosen from nos. 67–71.

Reading of the Word of God (Optional)

Then the priest may read or say from memory a text of Scripture which proclaims God's mercy and calls man to conversion.

A reading may also be chosen from those given in nos. 72–83 and 101–201 for the reconciliation of several penitents. The priest and penitent may choose other readings from scripture.

Confession of Sins and Acceptance of Satisfaction

Where it is the custom, the penitent says a general formula for confession (for example, **I confess to almighty God**) before he confesses his sins.

If necessary, the priest helps the penitent to make an integral confession and gives him suitable counsel. He urges him to be sorry for his faults, reminding him that through the sacrament of penance the Christian dies and rises with Christ and is thus renewed in the paschal mystery. The priest proposes an act of penance which the penitent accepts to make satisfaction for sin and to amend his life.

The priest should make sure that he adapts his counsel to the penitent's circumstances.

Prayer of the Penitent and Absolution

The priest then asks the penitent to express his sorrow, which the penitent may do in these or similar words:

My God,
I am sorry for my sins with all my heart.
In choosing to do wrong
and failing to do good,
I have sinned against you
whom I should love above all things.
I firmly intend, with your help,
to do penance,
to sin no more,
and to avoid whatever leads me to sin.
Our Savior Jesus Christ
suffered and died for us.
In his name, my God, have mercy.

Other prayers of the penitent may be chosen from nos. 85–92.

Or:

Lord Jesus, Son of God
have mercy on me, a sinner.

Absolution

Then the priest extends his hands over the penitent's head (or at least extends his right hand) and says:
> *God, the Father of mercies,*
> *through the death and resurrection of his Son*
> *has reconciled the world to himself*
> *and sent the Holy Spirit among us*
> *for the forgiveness of sins;*
> *through the ministry of the Church*
> *may God give you pardon and peace,*
> *and I absolve you from your sins*
> *in the name of the Father, and of the Son,* ✛
> *and of the Holy Spirit.*

The penitent answers:
Amen.

Proclamation of Praise of God and Dismissal

After the absolution, the priest continues:
Give thanks to the Lord, for he is good.

The penitent concludes:
His mercy endures for ever.

Then the priest dismisses the penitent who has been reconciled, saying:
The Lord has freed you from your sins. Go in peace.

Or [93]:
> *May the Passion of our Lord Jesus Christ,*
> *the intercession of the Blessed Virgin Mary, and of all*
> *the saints,*

whatever good you do and suffering you endure,
heal your sins,
help you to grow in holiness,
and reward you with eternal life.
Go in peace.

Or:
The Lord has freed you from sin.
May he bring you safely to his kingdom in heaven.
Glory to him for ever.
R:
Amen.
Or:
Blessed are those
whose sins have been forgiven,
whose evil deeds have been forgotten.
Rejoice in the Lord,
and go in peace.
Or:
Go in peace
and proclaim to the world
the wonderful works of God
who has brought you salvation.

APPENDIX C:
Small Group Faith Sharing Guide

The material in this book can be used in a parish setting in a variety of ways. It can be used in such programs as:

- Sacramental preparation classes
- RCIA
- Adult faith formation programs
- Book study clubs
- Prayer groups

How ever the material is used, it should be adapted to meet the unique needs of each individual parish. For example, there could be a single session or a series of sessions. The process that follows is for a series of four sessions. If choosing to use it for a single session, determine which aspects would be best for the group. We suggest that each session begin with a reflection and sharing on a scripture quote related to the theme of forgiveness. The participants should be asked to select the scripture quotes and lead the discussion. The individual leading the session might want to share the reason why he/she selected that specific quote.

The Process

The purpose of the sessions is twofold: to lead the participants toward making a decision to forgive someone for whom they have held a grievance, and to determine if they feel called to receive the sacrament of reconciliation.

The Sessions

Session One: Read chapters 1 and 2 and complete the section in chapter 1 which invites the readers to list their beliefs about forgiveness. This session would allow for discussion of the various beliefs that have emerged among the readers.

Session Two: Ask the participants to read as many of the vignettes as they wish. Then the participants would be asked to identify and explain which "face of forgiveness" touched them personally and why it did.

Session Three: Invite the participants to write their own "chapter" focusing on an experience of forgiveness or non-forgiveness in their own lives or in the lives of someone they know.

Session Four: Ask the participants to read chapters 28 and 29, as well as Appendices A and B prior to the meeting. In reading the material, they should be asked to focus on the following questions, which they will be invited to discuss at the session:

- What have been your experiences of the sacrament of penance and what are your attitudes and feelings about this sacrament?

- What do you see as the benefits of this sacrament?

- What questions do you have about the sacrament of penance?

BIBLIOGRAPHY

Broaddus, Cindy and Kimberly Lohman Suiters. *A Random Act: An Inspiring True Story of Fighting to Survive and Choosing to Forgive.* New York: William Morrow, 2005.

Campbell, Joseph. *Hero With a Thousand Faces.* Princeton, NJ: Princeton University Press, 1990.

Enright, Robert et al. *Interpersonal Forgiveness Within the Helping Professions: An Attempt to Resolve Differences of Opinions.* Unpublished document dated September, 1991.

Jenco, Lawrence Martin, O.S.M. *Bound to Forgive: The Pilgrimage to Reconciliation of a Beirut Hostage.* Notre Dame, IN: Ave Maria Press, 1995.

Lewis, Gregg and Debbie Morris. *Forgiving the Dead Man Walking.* Grand Rapids: Zondervan Publishing, 1998.

Libreria Editrice Vaticana. *Catechism of the Catholic Church, second edition.* Washington, DC: USCCB Publishing, 1997.

Menninger, Karl. *Whatever Became of Sin.* New York: Hawthorne Books, 1973.

Nouwen, Henri. *The Wounded Healer.* Garden City, NY: Image Books, 1979.

Pope John Paul II. *The Mission of the Redeemer.* Boston: Pauline Books and Media, 1990.

———. "No Peace Without Justice: No Justice Without Forgiveness." World Day of Peace Message. January 1, 2002.

Smedes, Lewis B. *Forgive and Forget.* San Francisco: Harper and Row. 1984.

Sofield, Loughlan, Rosine Hammett, and Carroll Juliano. *Building Community: Christian, Caring, Vital.* Notre Dame, IN: Ave Maria Press, 1998.

———. *Design for Wholeness: Dealing With Anger, Learning to Forgive, Building Self-Esteem.* Notre Dame, IN: Ave Maria Press, 1990.

Time, "I Spoke as a Brother: A Pardon from the Pontiff; A Message of Forgiveness to a Troubled World," January 7, 1984.

United States Conference of Catholic Bishops. *Stewardship: A Disciple's Response.* Washington, DC: United States Catholic Conference of Bishops Publishing, 1993.

USA Today, "What Makes People Happy: Psychologists Now Know," December 9, 2002.

van Breemen, Peter. *The God Who Won't Let Go.* Notre Dame, IN: Ave Maria Press, 2001.

Brother Loughlan Sofield, S.T., a member of the Missionary Servants of the Most Holy Trinity, has been a Brother for fifty years. Sofield spends most of his time "on the road," conducting workshops, giving presentations, and facilitating groups all over the world.

Sister Carroll Juliano, S.H.C.J., a member of the Leadership Team of the American Province of the Sisters of the Holy Child Jesus, is an award-winning author who conducts workshops throughout the world. She served as an advisor and consultant to the United States Conference of Catholic Bishops' Committee on Women in Society and in the Church.

Sofield and Juliano are co-authors (with Rosine Hammett) of *Collaboration: Uniting Our Gifts in Ministry; Design for Wholeness: Dealing with Anger, Learning to Forgive, Building Self-Esteem;* and *Building Community: Christian, Caring, Vital* (Ave Maria Press).

Bishop Gregory M. Aymond was ordained to the priesthood in 1975 in the Archdiocese of New Orleans. His years of ministry include serving on the staff of Notre Dame Seminary Graduate School of Theology where he also spent fourteen years as the Rector/President. In 1997, Pope John Paul II appointed him Auxiliary Bishop of the Archdiocese of New Orleans. Bishop Aymond assumed his current post as Bishop of Austin, Texas, in 2001.